Writings
on
China

Gottfried Wilhelm Leibniz

Writings on China

*Translated, with an
Introduction, Notes, and
Commentaries
by*

Daniel J. Cook
and
Henry Rosemont, Jr.

OPEN ✹ COURT

Chicago and La Salle, Illinois

Map of Asia from Guillaume Delisle: L' Asie. Paris, 1700.

An earlier edition of a part of this book was published in 1977 by the University Press of Hawaii under the title: *Discourse on the Natural Theology of the Chinese.*

© 1994 by Open Court Publishing Company

First printing 1994

Printed and bound in the United States of America.

Library of Congress Cataloging-in-Publication Data

Leibniz, Gottfried Wilhelm, Freiherr von, 1646–1716.
    [Selections. English. 1994]
    Writings on China / translated, with an introduction, notes, and commentaries by Daniel J. Cook and Henry Rosemont, Jr.
      p.   cm.
    A collection of four pieces originally written in Latin and French.
    Includes bibliographical references and index.
    ISBN 0-8126-9250-0.—ISBN 0-8126-9251-9 (pbk.)
    1. Philosophy, Chinese. 2. Confucianism. I. Cook, Daniel J.
II. Rosemont, Henry, 1934–   . III. Title.
B2599.C5L45213 1994
181'. 11—dc20
                                              94-29940
                                                CIP

Daniel J. Cook wishes to dedicate his work in this volume to his wife, Miri, and his children, Sarah, Eli, and Benjy.

Henry Rosemont, Jr., wishes to dedicate his work in this volume to his mother, Sally Rosemont, and to the memory of his father, Henry P. Rosemont.

Contents

Illustrations

GOTTFRIED WILHELM VON LEIBNITZ

1646 - 1716

AFTER A PICTURE IN THE FLORENCE LIBRARY

Plate 1. Gottfried Wilhelm Leibniz (from *A Portfolio of Eminent Mathematicians*, ed. by David Eugene Smith [Chicago: Open Court, 1896])

Preface

Although Gottfried Wilhelm Leibniz is best known as a metaphysician, mathematician, and logician, he arguably used the word "China" in his voluminous writings and correspondence more often than those terms usually associated with him: "entelechies," "monads," "pre-established harmony," and so forth. If so, then his sustained writings on things Chinese—especially on Chinese philosophy and religion—should take their place alongside his other major works such as the *Theodicy, Discourse on Metaphysics, Monadology,* and the *New Essays Concerning Human Understanding.*[1]

His more detailed writings on China (as opposed to brief references to it, which he regularly made in his correspondence) can be roughly divided into two categories. The first is the letters he wrote to European—usually Jesuit—missionaries in China, or their peers in Europe. Especially is this true of his correspondence with Joachim Bouvet, one of the first French Jesuits to live in China, and whose letters to Leibniz clearly influenced the philosopher. (For more on Bouvet, see below, p. 16). All of these letters have now been published—although not translated—by Dr. Rita Widmaier in *Leibniz Korrespondiert mit China,*[2] and it is our hope that this entire correspondence will soon be presented in an English edition (particularly the Leibniz–Bouvet letters, which are philosophically the most significant).

The second category of Leibniz's sustained writings on sinological topics are the four texts presented herein. The first was written expressly for publication, which Leibniz seldom did; the second and third were written as brief essays on Chinese thought, and then sent as appendices to letters to a few among his numerous correspondents. And the fourth is a lengthy treatise on Chinese natural theology, which he wrote the year he died, to be sent as a letter to the same correspondent to whom he had addressed the *Monadology* two years earlier.

Thus, while these four texts are by no means a complete inventory of

Leibniz's China writings, we do believe that collectively they provide a fairly comprehensive view of what he had to say about things Chinese, and that they provide a number of insights into Leibniz's own philosophy as well.

We have attempted to provide enough introductory materials for readers to both situate themselves in the Europe of Leibniz's day, and to understand the Chinese history, beliefs, and terms that Leibniz describes, analyzes, and evaluates in his writings. These introductory materials have been supplemented at length by references and commentaries footnoted in the translations themselves.

Probably the most influential modern book on Leibniz's views has been Bertrand Russell's *A Critical Exposition of the Philosophy of Leibniz*,[3] in which Russell charges Leibniz with "insincerity" because of the seeming (to Russell) chasm separating Leibniz's logic and metaphysics from his theology. More recently, however, this view of Leibniz has been called into question. In concluding his *The Philosophy of Leibniz* (which does not mention China at all), Nicholas Rescher says:

> Leibniz eagerly wanted to persuade his readers (usually his correspondents), not in order to win personal disciples in high places, but to secure effective adherents to implement a vision of truths which he felt capable of healing the theological strifes and political discords in Europe of his day. Had fame been his prime goal he would have written more books and fewer letters. What Leibniz wanted was not public acclaim, but influential converts who could implement in the sphere of action his reconciling insights in the sphere of thought. It is always risky to speculate on motives, but in my own mind there is no doubt that the aspirations which actuated him were, in the main, not those of selfishness but of public spirit.[4]

We believe that after going through Leibniz's China writings, readers will appreciate that Rescher, not Russell, has taken the more accurate measure of one of the greatest thinkers of Western civilization, and one of the very few among those greats who attempted to see beyond its confines.

Notes

1. A full reference for each of these—and other works of Leibniz—is given in the Bibliography.

2. Frankfurt am Main: Vittorio Klostermann, 1990.

3. Cambridge: Cambridge University Press, 1900.

4. Englewood Cliffs, NJ: Prentice-Hall, 1967, p. 160.

Acknowledgments

The scope of Leibniz's knowledge, interests and ideas expressed in his writings on China is intellectually forbidding. Virtually no one scholar—or even two—trained today could comment intelligently on everything in this corpus. We therefore had to request and secure a good deal of assistance.

Our greatest debt is to Donald F. Lach, Professor of History Emeritus at the University of Chicago, whose work in this field is invaluable. We are grateful for his permission to republish, with only minor changes, his long out-of-print *The Preface to NOVISSIMA SINICA.*

Dr. Rita Widmaier of the Leibniz Archives of the Lower Saxony State Library in Hannover, Germany has (1) provided us with drafts of her unpublished German translations of *De cultu Confucii civili* and what we have entitled *Remarks on Chinese Rites and Religion;* (2) answered a number of textual and factual questions; and (3) published two scholarly volumes in German on Leibniz's writings about China, from which we have drawn with profit. We also wish to thank the late Director of the Leibniz Archives, Professor Albert Heinekamp, as well as the present one, Dr. Herbert Breger, for their on-going support and assistance. Ms. Anke Hoelzer of the Manuscripts Section of the Library supplied us with needed copies of many original editions and documents of Leibniz.

Although Professor David Mungello of Coe College did not see the present work in draft form, he did comment in detail on our earlier translation of the *Discourse,* and his recent work, *Curious Land,* as well as his earlier book, *Leibniz and Confucianism,* are probably the most frequently cited secondary sources we have used.

We are also grateful to Ms. Claudia von Collani of Wuerzburg, Germany, for kindly assisting us with several historical details. We have profited from her meticulous research during the period dealt with in the book.

At St. Mary's College of Maryland, we owe a great debt to Ms. Gail Dean for her beautifully typed manuscript of our Introduction and to Ms.

Linda Vallandingham for her masterful transcription of our translations of the Leibniz texts. Both have been a joy to work with throughout. We give special thanks to Constance Rosemont, who prepared the index in a thorough and wide-ranging manner.

We are also grateful to the editorial staff of Open Court, particularly David Ramsay Steele, Kerri Mommer and Edward Roberts, for their support, assistance, and encouragement. We owe a special thanks to our copy editor, Richard Weisenseel, who worked well with a manuscript containing materials in six languages. We also salute the memory of the founder of Open Court, Paul Carus, who, like a latter-day Leibniz, devoted much of his life to promoting cross-cultural philosophical understanding.

We are deeply thankful to all these people; much that may be good or useful in this book is due to them. For what is less good and useful, readers should not fear that each of us will attempt to blame the other: the bonds of respect and affection that have matured over our many years of collaboration insure that we will jointly accept responsibility for all shortcomings.

We completed the final draft of this work while at opposite ends of the Asian continent, living in the lands which are physically and spiritually the birthplaces of the two traditions—the Judeo-Christian and the Confucian —which Leibniz worked so hard to reconcile.

Tel Aviv/Shanghai   D.J.C.
May, 1994   H.R.

康熙

Plate 2. The emperor Kang Xi (from the frontispiece of Father Bouvet's book)

L'ASIE

Dressée sur les Observations de l'Academie
Royale des Sciences et quelques autres, et sur
les memoires les plus recens.
Par G. de l'Isle Geographe.

A PARIS
Chez l'Auteur Rue des Canettes prez de
St. Sulpice Avec Privilege du Roy
pour 20 Ans 1700.

ECHELLE

Lieues communes d'Allemagne
Lieues marines d'Espagne
Parasanges de Perse
Cosses des Etats du Mogol
Verstes de Moscovie
Lieues ou Stadts de la Chine
Lieues du Japon
Journées communes

MER GLACIALE

LAPONIE

EUROPE

POLOGNE

MOSCOVIE

TARTARIE MO

GRAND

TARTARIE IND

CALMOUCS

TURQUIE EUROPE NE TARTARIE

GRECE

MER NOIRE

CIRCASSIE

MER CASPIEN

CHORASAN

TURQUE

TURQUIE EUROP.

NATOLIE
TURQUIE ASIATIQUE

ARMENIE
CURDI

PERSE

MER MEDITERRANÉE

EGYPTE

ARABIE DESERTA

GOLFE PERSIQUE

SEGESTAN

MECRAN

ETATS DU GRA

NUBIE

MER ROUGE

ARABIE

ARABIE HEUREUSE

YEMEN

MAHRE

R. DE GAOGA

R. DE GORHAN

ABISSINIE

AFRIQUE

AJAN

Magadoxo

Melinde

I. de Socotora

ISLES MALDIVES

MER DES I

Equateur ou Ligne Equinoctiale

AVERTISSEMENT

Comme il y a plusieurs choses sur cette Carte et
sur les autres que j'ay mises au jour qui sont
differentes de ce qui se trouve sur les Cartes
qui ont paru jusqu'icy. Il est a propos d'avertir
icy que cela n'est point arrivé par inadvertence
et que je rends raison de ces changemens dans
la Nouvelle Introduction a la Geographie.

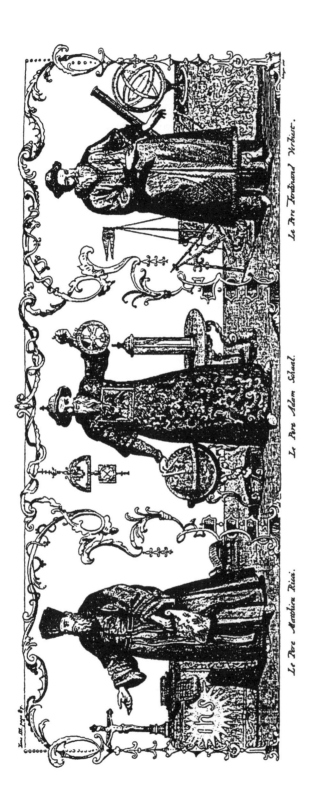

Plate 4. Ricci, Schall, and Verbiest (from Du Halde's *Description . . . de la Chine*)

Introduction

I. *The Background of Leibniz's China Writings*

If Erasmus of Rotterdam was the "Universal Man" of the late fifteenth and early sixteenth centuries, Gottfried Wilhelm Leibniz was a major candidate for the title two hundred years later. He not only studied, but wrote original works on subjects as diverse as geometry and biology, geology and theology, and metaphysics and statistics; he was one of the foremost mathematicians of his time, and a famous philosopher whose fame has endured; and he was all of these while engaged in a long and active public career.[1]

Born in Leipzig in 1646, Leibniz entered the university there fifteen years later, then studied at Jena, and then at the University of Altdorf, where he received his doctorate in law. After a succession of posts, and years in Paris (1672–1676), Leibniz became a councillor and librarian to the Duke of Hanover, the position he held until his death in 1716. His proximity to an important German court gave Leibniz a certain amount of political influence which, when coupled with his manifold intellectual achievements—the infinitesimal calculus, binary arithmetic, philosophical writings—made him one of the most important and well-known intellectuals of his time, seen clearly by the very large number of people eager, pleased, and flattered to meet him, and to engage him in correspondence.

And Leibniz was a prolific correspondent: to this day there is no complete inventory of all his writings. Among his more well-known regular correspondents were Antoine Arnauld, Samuel Clarke, Christian Wolff, Christian Huygens, Nicolas Malebranche—among the intelligentsia—and a fairly large and diverse group of councillors and diplomats, kings and queens, emperors and empresses.[2]

In addition, Leibniz engaged in lengthy correspondence with a number of clergymen, especially Jesuits, and a common topic in their exchanges of letters was China. It is well known that things Chinese interested Leibniz throughout his life, and a number of his clerical correspondents were missionaries to the "Middle Kingdom," among them probably the most knowledgeable Europeans of their day on China. He was keenly interested in virtually everything about China: history, geography, language, flora and fauna, technology, and of course philosophy and religion; at the time of his death, he probably knew as much about the country and its people as anyone who had not actually been there.

This dimension of Leibniz's intellectual life has been investigated by a number of historians and sinologists, but has been almost totally neglected by later philosophers, who have focused instead (and almost solely) on his work in logic, mathematics, and ontology.[3] But his Chinese writings must be addressed by all serious Leibnizians, and scholars of seventeenth and eighteenth century Europe, because the bibliographic evidence indicates that he mentions China more often in his writings than all other non-Western cultures combined. Why China? Why not Muslim culture(s) to which he refers on occasion? Or India? Or the "Indians" of the New World about whom books were being written and circulated in Europe while Leibniz was still a relatively young man?[4]

To answer these questions we must first appreciate Leibniz's central metaphysical vision. Rejecting the dualism of Descartes and the monism of Spinoza, Leibniz instead stressed plurality, diversity, harmony, and a higher-order unity that could be grasped by reason, and expressed in a logically perfect language purged of all ambiguities. Like Spinoza, Leibniz held that substances could not interact. The former concluded that there could therefore be only a single substance, but the latter instead argued for an indefinitely large number of them. These substances, which Leibniz late in his life called "monads," were self-contained, and while they could not causally affect others of their kind, they could all dance to the same tune played in a pre-established harmony composed by God.

This metaphysical vision has often been referred to as an organic philosophy,[5] in contrast to the mechanistic views of Descartes and Galileo. It is original with Leibniz—although parts of it can be traced to Giordano Bruno and Nicholas Cusanus, and through them (plus others) to the Hermetic tradition—and because it bears a close resemblance to the Chinese metaphysical view of the world, it has been claimed that Leibniz's philosophy was deeply indebted to Chinese thought.[6] This claim does not withstand close scrutiny; the textual evidence suggests strongly that

Chinese thought did not influence directly Leibniz's metaphysical vision. Nevertheless, in finding views approximating his own in a culture 3,000 years and 8,000 miles distant from him, Leibniz could not but be interested in, stimulated by, and sympathetic to early Chinese thought as he had come to understand it.[7]

At the same time, Leibniz's public life was a political one. He wished to reconcile Catholics and Protestants, and to halt the internecine strife plaguing the European states of his day. He believed that China could assist in achieving this goal, his writings displaying the following pattern of reasoning: my philosophy is fully compatible with those elements of Christian theology on which there is a large measure of agreement between Catholics and Protestants; my philosophy is fully compatible with (early) basic beliefs of the Chinese; therefore Chinese basic beliefs are fully compatible with those basic beliefs shared by Catholic and Protestants, and therefore in turn those Christian doctrines in dispute between Catholics and Protestants should be seen as relatively unimportant in the larger scheme of things, and can be adjudicated to the satisfaction of all on the basis of reason—with a resultant international peace and harmony among and between all of the world's peoples.

But harmony was not even to be found in Europe during Leibniz's time, and China was a major focus of dispute, both theological and political.

Theologically there were two burning questions which divided the missionaries to China, and the divisions quickly spread back to Europe. The first of these was whether the Chinese language did or did not contain a close lexical equivalent for the Christian "God." If not, it must follow that the Chinese were all atheists. The Jesuit founder of the mission in China, Matteo Ricci, allowed two terms from the Chinese: *Shang Di*—"Supreme Ancestor"—and *Tian*—"Heaven"—as equivalents for "God," and himself used another, *Tian Zhu,* "Heaven's Lord."[8] Many later missionaries, however, disputed *Shang Di* and *Tian* as translations for "God," claiming that the Chinese terms had connotations inconsistent with the Christian concept of deity. (And these latter missionaries later carried the day, with *Tian Zhu* becoming the official Catholic term for "God" in Chinese.)

This controversy paralleled another, even more intense one—the so-called "Rites Controversy." In this case the question was whether the rites carried out by all Chinese to their ancestors, and by many Chinese to Confucius, were basically civic and secular in nature, or idolatrous and superstition-ridden. If the former (Ricci's view), then there was no harm done in permitting their continuance among Christian converts. But if the latter, then of course the Chinese would have to abandon these rituals altogether as a precondition for baptism into the true faith.

Most (but not all) Jesuits adopted Ricci's conciliatory stance toward Chinese ritual practices, while the great majority of the Franciscans and Dominicans who followed the Jesuits to China did not. In the strict theological sense—with respect to the Chinese—the Friars' arguments are now seen to have been the better ones: there is nothing remotely resembling Genesis in Chinese texts, there is no conception of a divine lawgiver, and the Passion of Christ had to strike virtually every educated Chinese as incredible, repugnant, or both. On the other hand, it can now equally be seen that the Fathers (Jesuits) were certainly correct to resist insisting that candidates for conversion give up cultural practices over three millennia old; without accommodation, China would remain forever "heathen."

Complicating these religious controversies were political ones, as budding nation states sought empire. The Jesuits came from a variety of ethnic backgrounds but worked in China under the general jurisdiction of the Portuguese, entering the Middle Kingdom via Goa and Macao. Dominicans and Franciscans, however, were under the patronage of the Spanish crown, and endeavored to enter the country from the Philippines. China thus became contested territory for evangelical efforts, because where missionaries go, merchants will follow and colonies can be established, all of which can enlarge the coffers of the imperial court.

Against this brief metaphysical, theological, and political background we may now place the writings of Leibniz on China gathered together in this volume. One of the relatively few of his works on any subject published during his lifetime was his *Preface to the NOVISSIMA SINICA* (*Recent News from China*), issued in 1697, and, slightly revised, again in 1699—hereafter referred to as the *Preface*. It is a diverse body of writings, largely by missionaries to China, that Leibniz gathered together, editing some and translating others, basically to serve his ecumenical interests. Given his great reluctance to publish anything, Leibniz's presentation of this book and *Preface* indicates that those ecumenical interests were very important to him.

The work deals largely with the Rites Controversy, the role of Muscovy (Russia) as an intermediary between China and Europe, and the consequent need for a land route through Russia between the former and the latter. It also gives information about missionary diplomatic missions, activities, and travels, and stresses as well the need for Protestant missions in China. Although Leibniz evinces clear sympathies with Jesuit views on these matters, he is always the discreet diplomat himself, finding something good to say about almost everyone mentioned in the text, and at all times stressing the need to seek harmony between competing European groups, and between all Europeans and the Russians, and the Chinese.[9]

A year after the publication of the second edition of *NOVISSIMA SINICA* Leibniz wrote an addendum to a letter to Father Antoine Verjus (1632–1706), procurator of the missions to India and China. He entitled the addendum *De cultu Confucii civili* (*On the Civil Cult of Confucius;* hereafter *De cultu*). Here again he sides with the Jesuits on the Rites Controversy, and comments as well on the other theological dispute, the "Terms Controversy."

During the same year (1700) the Jesuits—especially the French Jesuits who began missionary efforts in China toward the end of the 1600s—got into trouble with the Faculty of the Sorbonne, who concluded lengthy deliberations on two popular texts supportive of the Jesuit position(s) by condemning them. These two works, authored by the Fathers Louis Le Comte (1655–1728)[10] and Charles Le Gobien (1653–1708),[11] made claims that Leibniz endorsed, among them: (1) that the Chinese had knowledge of God two thousand years before the time of Christ; (2) that God had constantly favored China; (3) that the Chinese should not, therefore, view Christianity as a foreign religion. The Sorbonne Faculty, largely Jansenist, did not take kindly—at the political level—to these attacks on Eurocentrism, nor at the doctrinal level did they appreciate the anti-Augustinian implications of these views. St. Augustine saw grace as necessary for overcoming human sinfulness; most Jesuits, following Augustine's theological opponent Pelagius, saw it as sufficient but not necessary. Succinctly stated:

> The Jesuits interpreted the Bible as a spiritual guide to completing God's work in the world rather than as a book which told a story of salvation whose geographical and cultural limits had already been reached. Consequently, they saw China as a part of God's plan for salvation.[12]

But the Sorbonne Faculty did not. Their condemnation of the works of Le Comte and Le Gobien did not come until October 1700, which was ten months after Leibniz dated *De cultu*. But it is clear both from that work and from his *Preface* that he knew of Le Comte's and Le Gobien's works, and he should have had intimations of the brewing theological and political storm and therefore perhaps composed both works to weigh in, gently but clearly, on the side that ultimately lost.

The third of Leibniz's China writings included in this volume is presented for the first time in English translation. From 1706 until his death, Leibniz corresponded with Bartholomaeus des Bosses (1668–1728), who taught at the Jesuit college in Hildesheim. In one of Leibniz's missives, dated 12 August 1709,[13] he said he was also including a copy of some remarks he had written a year earlier on Chinese rites and religion. This text—hereafter cited as *Remarks*—is relatively brief, but it is nevertheless the most sustained discussion of Chinese philosophy and religion that Leibniz had written up to that time in his life. While ecumenical and political issues can be discerned in the text, its primary thrust is philosophical and religious. In it Leibniz displays the influence of his correspondence with Jesuit missionaries in China and presents as well what he took to be the relevance of his binary arithmetic to understanding (ancient) Chinese thought.

Many of the ideas adumbrated only briefly in the *Remarks* receive more comprehensive treatment in a work he called a "Discours sur la Théologie naturelle des Chinois" (hereafter referred to as the *Discourse*). Not until the last year of his life did he set down his views on Chinese philosophy and religion systematically, in a long letter written to one of his later correspondents, Nicholas de Rémond, a French Platonist and the head of the councils of the Duke of Orleans. Along with a letter written the year before (1715), Rémond sent Leibniz two works on Chinese religion written by Catholic missionaries who had lived and worked there, and asked the philosopher's opinion of them.[14] Both of these works were hostile to the general Jesuit position (even though one of them was written by a Jesuit; see below, p. 14). Leibniz had read reviews of these two works, and mentioned them—graciously but unapprovingly—in the *Remarks;*[15] he must have decided, in response to Rémond's query, that it was time to take up in detail a sustained philosophical and theological defense of the dominant Jesuit views, which he saw as needed for his ecumenical concerns.

Even by Leibnizian standards (and he was a prolific correspondent) his reply to Rémond is a long one, over 14,000 words. The main topics discussed are the Chinese conceptions of God, universal principles, spiritual substance(s), souls, immortality, and early Chinese ideas. In these contexts he also discusses his own famous views of pre-established harmony, entelechies, primary and secondary matter, and God. (The terminology of the monads is alone missing, which is especially odd, since the text now known as the *Monadology,* written in 1714, was actually another letter written to the same correspondent, Rémond.)

For the most part, Leibniz describes his position and advances his arguments in the *Discourse* clearly enough to be followed without undue difficulty. Nevertheless, a brief overview of the work may be useful at the outset, because the several historical, philosophical, and political issues at stake were not as clearly delimited by Leibniz as a modern reader might desire, owing in large measure to the fact that he was not only outlining his own views, but responding to the views of others.

The two missionary texts make the same arguments with respect to Chinese thought. According to their authors, resemblances between Chinese and Christian concepts were only superficial, especially on issues basic to Christian theology: (1) the nature of God, and spiritual substance(s); (2) the existence and qualities of spirits, and matter; and (3) the immortality of the human soul. In the opinion of the missionaries, the ancient Chinese thinkers were, at best, materialists; and even this much could not be said for their modern counterparts, who were simply atheists. To support their positions the missionaries cited passages from classical texts, passages from commentaries thereon, and they also quoted at length contemporary Chinese intellectuals (some of them Christian converts) with whom they had spoken. This evidence was placed (according to Leibniz)[16] in a Scholastic philosophical framework, from which their negative theological conclusions were generated. And these conclusions in turn generated a more political one, equally negative: because Christian doctrine is incompatible with Chinese thought, the conversion of the Chinese can only proceed by having them abandon altogether their intellectual and cultural heritage in favor of revealed Christian truth.

The *Discourse* is an attempt to counter this position philosophically and at the most general structural level should be read as an argument *modus tollens.* The conclusion—that conversion of the Chinese requires abandonment of a 3,000-year-old intellectual tradition—must be false; therefore the premise(s) from which the conclusion follows must also be false.

There are four sections[17] in the *Discourse,* the first three of which contain Leibniz's detailed replies to the missionaries' claims that Chinese thought is fundamentally incompatible with basic Christian doctrines. He first argues (part I) that the Chinese do indeed have a close conceptual analogue to the Christian concept of God, and spiritual substance. In part II, which is almost half of the manuscript, Leibniz maintains that spirits and matter in China are considered and treated in very nearly the same way angels and matter are considered and treated in Christian Europe. Part III is devoted to making a similar case for the compatibility of the Chinese and Christian concepts of the human soul and its immortality.[18]

Together the first three parts comprise over nine-tenths of the *Discourse*. Part IV appears to be more or less an appendix to it, the subject under discussion being an exposition of Leibniz's binary arithmetic, and an analogue with it claimed by Leibniz and his French Jesuit correspondent in China, Joachim Bouvet, to be found in the trigrams of the *Yi Jing*, or *Book of Changes*. Part IV is not, however, an appendix. On the contrary, it is an essential ingredient of Leibniz's most fundamental argument, and it must be seen as such in order to appreciate Leibniz's overall view of the nature, history, and development of Chinese thought.

He accepts, for the most part, the claims of the anti-Riccians that many educated Chinese of his own time were atheists. But, he insists, these moderns have "strayed . . . from their own antiquity" (§1). If we focus instead on the classical texts, he says, "I find [them] quite excellent, and quite in accord with natural theology. . . . It is pure Christianity, insofar as it renews the natural law inscribed in our hearts" (§31).

To be sure, there are important theological issues on which the classical texts are silent, and even the most famous of Chinese philosophers, Confucius, is occasionally in "error."[19] But this only shows, Leibniz believed, that we have not gone back far enough in the relevant cases. If we return to the era of the sage-kings, "we could uncover in the Chinese writings of the remotest antiquity many things unknown to modern Chinese and *even to those commentators thought to be classical*" (§68; emphasis added). The *Yi Jing* is one such book, according to him, and if we read it carefully, what we will uncover is the fact that "the ancient Chinese have surpassed the modern ones in the extreme, not only in piety . . . but in science as well" (§68a).

The crucial term in this quote is "science," which is why part IV is crucial to the *Discourse*: "it concerns justification of the doctrines of the ancient Chinese and their superiority over the moderns" (§69). Remember that Leibniz acknowledged the theological weaknesses of modern Chinese thinkers, but maintained that the ancient texts—some of them pre-

Confucian—strongly suggested a natural theology consonant with Christianity, and thereby worthy of European respect. What better way to establish that respect than to show that the most ancient authors of those texts not only had theological ideas similar to Christian theology but also developed pure mathematics to a point which had only been reached in Europe during his own lifetime? Leibniz believed (as did Bouvet) that while binary arithmetic was not the "universal characteristic" he had long sought, it was nevertheless the basis of natural science.[20] If he could show, therefore—to post-Galilean Europe—that his mathematical notation had been prefigured 4,500 years earlier in China, Leibniz would have a very strong case for denying the conclusion of the two missionaries and for advancing his own view of the proper method for engaging the Chinese in ecumenical dialogue: show them the truth, but not simply by quoting from the Bible and giving them telescopes; show them also how both theological and scientific truth could be read in their most ancient writings. This argument also provided Leibniz with an explanation for the silence of Confucius on some important theological issues, and his "mistakes" on others; he, too, had occasionally lost the meaning(s) of the writings of his predecessors, and therefore could not be relied upon uniformly as the ultimate authority on, of, or for Chinese thought.[21]

Seen in this light, part IV of the *Discourse* can be read as the *coup de grace* to the anti-accommodationist position with respect to China. The text breaks off abruptly, and although Leibniz continued to write for the remaining months of his life, he never returned to the *Discourse* to finish it. The evidence suggests, however, that philosophically the manuscript may be substantively complete and that Leibniz had accomplished what he had set out to do: provide a sophisticated philosophical and theological framework in which the ecumenical movement in China could go forward.

The *Discourse* should thus be seen as an attempt on Leibniz's part to (1) show the universality of his philosophical views; (2) demonstrate the harmony of his views with Christian doctrine, and of both with Chinese beliefs; and (3) to defend, with all of the powerful intellectual resources he commanded, the dominant Jesuit position in the Rites Controversy and other disputes. His efforts, and those of the Jesuits, ultimately failed; the controversies were eventually settled against the Jesuits by Benedict XIV's *Ex quo singulari* of 1742. Thus the Jesuits lost the ideological struggle, and their opponents in turn "lost" the conversion of the Chinese, as history unfolded; how much these losses were to be of significance is still a matter of dispute both within and without the Vatican. Had he lived that long,

Leibniz would have been bitterly disappointed at the papal decision, as his China writings make clear, and as he emphasized in a letter written in 1710: "In the Chinese controversy which is raging at Rome today, I favor the Jesuits and have for a long time . . ."[22]

Three centuries have passed since Leibniz began his efforts to promote greater understanding between China and the West, and it is not cynical to suggest that there has not been a great deal of progress toward the goal. The vision of Leibniz for a close understanding and communication between China and the West has not yet come to realization. The growth of knowledge of Chinese culture in the United States and Europe has not been matched by a similar growth in its dissemination, especially at the public level; and the respectability of narrow specialization in the academic disciplines provides a ready-made excuse for all but China scholars to professionally ignore the world's oldest continuous culture, inherited by one quarter of the human race. Given the economic, political, social, and philosophical crises currently facing the Western capitalist democracies, it might well be salutary to look beyond our own cultural traditions for new—or very old—intellectual horizons, as Leibniz did.

In this light we would do well to heed the prophetic remark made by Leibniz in a letter to Tsar Peter the Great in 1716, the same year he composed the *Discourse*. If we do not actively promote understanding, exchange, and communication between the Chinese and ourselves, he said,

> It will follow that when the Chinese will have learnt from us what they wish to know they will then close their doors to us.[23]

The Chinese writings of Leibniz should therefore be read by all students of his work because of what he said in them. And they deserve a wider audience as well because they represent the sustained efforts of one gifted man to bring about universal harmony between the varied peoples of this earth. Leibniz attempted to keep a Western foot in the Chinese door and to open it wider so that we might all look in.

II. *Sources of Leibniz's Knowledge of China*

Almost totally ignorant of China for a thousand years, Europe began to receive a trickle of information about the "Middle Kingdom" again at the close of the thirteenth century, beginning with the dissemination of the journals of Marco Polo and his brothers. Nevertheless, knowledge of China was still rather fragmentary in Leibniz's Europe four hundred years later. There were few translations of Chinese texts, the language was considered exotic, communications were poor and infrequent, and myths about the land and its peoples abounded.[24] The earliest mention of China in the Leibniz corpus appears to date from 1668, with Leibniz comparing Chinese medicine favorably to Europe's:

> No matter how foolish and paradoxical the Chinese ordinarily appear to be in *re medica*, nevertheless, theirs is better than ours.[25]

In his early days, however, the philosopher was not uniformly approbationary in his remarks on China. In his *Consilium Aegyptiacum*, written in 1671–72, Leibniz mentions China over a dozen times, dwelling on Chinese corruption, misuse of its wealth, and

> their million soldiers who guarded in vain their wondrous wall . . . vanquished by 60,000 enemy soldiers . . . and recently submitted to the yoke of the Tartars.[26]

Leibniz's first reference to Chinese thought is in 1670, in a letter to the German Jesuit Athanasius Kircher (1601–1680).[27] The letter, however, merely evinces an interest in the latter's writings on China; it does not suggest that Leibniz knew anything himself about the subject at that time.

By 1679 it is clear that Leibniz had some knowledge of the structure of the Chinese written language. In January of that year, he learned of the efforts of Andreas Müller (1630?–1694) to work a "key" to written Chinese, and in June wrote a letter to Müller asking a number of sophisticated questions about the language and the latter's work on it.[28] Müller claimed to have devised a *Clavis Sinica* ("Key to Chinese"), but never published it, nor would he provide any details of his work to Leibniz, or to any of his other correspondents. In the *Preface*, Leibniz describes Müller's temperament as "peculiar," and bemoans the fact that Müller never made his work available to others.

Similarly, Leibniz was aware at this relatively early time of the view of the Dutch scholar Jacob Gohl (Jacobus Golius) that Chinese had been invented all at once,[29] and was aware as well of the work of the Englishman John Webb, who had published a book—a copy of which is still in Leibniz's library—which endeavored to establish Chinese as the "primitive language" of the human race.[30] Later, Leibniz would be in correspondence with Christian Mentzel (1622–1701) who also claimed to have, but never published, a *Clavis Sinica*.[31]

Throughout the 1670s and early 1680s a group of Jesuit missionaries in China had been compiling a history of China, translating a few classical texts, analyzing the language, and much else. Their work was published in 1687 under the title *Confucius Sinarum philosophus sive scientia Sinensis latine exposita,* edited by the Belgian Father Philippe Couplet (1623–1693).[32] In a December letter of the same year written to the Landgrave, Ernst von Hessen-Rheinfels, Leibniz indicated that he has read through the Couplet work,[33] but he seldom mentions it in his later correspondence, and no mention of it at all is made in the *Discourse,* just as there are no references therein to any of the works of Kircher, Müller, Gohl, or Webb.

The beginning of Leibniz's mature study and knowledge of things Chinese is best dated to 1689, when he was in Rome, and met Claudio Grimaldi (1638–1712). Grimaldi, a Jesuit, was born in Northern Italy and took priestly vows when he was nineteen. Entering China as a missionary in 1669, he soon found his way to the court of Beijing and, with Ferdinand Verbiest, S.J. (1623–1688), served as a diplomatic aide to the Chinese emperor, and became active in the mathematical and astronomical endeavors at court. After seventeen years there, he returned to Rome and met Leibniz.[34]

Following this meeting, Leibniz addressed thirty questions about China to Grimaldi in a letter written in July of the same year.[35] The questions ranged from the industrial arts to botany, from chemistry to military weapons; they reflect Leibniz's encyclopedic interests but reflect as well that at the time of writing, he was not well versed in Chinese history, geography, or culture. Even at this early stage of his sinological development, however, Leibniz displayed the concerns that motivated his later studies, and which found expression in all of his substantive writings on China: the importance of learning about China for Europe's benefit, and the desire to increase Chinese receptivity to European ideas and artifacts—both concerns having as their goal the closer cooperation, understanding, and intercourse between the two civilizations. (Leibniz once referred to China as an "Oriental Europe."[36])

In answering Leibniz's questions Grimaldi disparaged to some extent —not entirely accurately—Chinese astronomical abilities, which probably formed the basis of the philosopher's fairly low opinion of the current state of the natural sciences in China.[37] Leibniz held Grimaldi in high regard, partly because of the latter's scientific skills, and partly because of

Grimaldi's close association with Verbiest, who was also a competent scientist but, more important for Leibniz's ecumenical interests, was influential at the Chinese court.

For these reasons, Leibniz remained in correspondence with Grimaldi for several years after returning to Hanover, and both Grimaldi and Verbiest contributed to the *NOVISSIMA SINICA*. Grimaldi's influence on Leibniz was not, however, confined to his knowledge of Chinese flora and fauna; the missionary also held definite views about Chinese philosophy and religion, views first put forth by the most famous of all missionaries to China: Matteo Ricci.[38]

Ricci was born in 1552 in Macerata, Italy, and attended Jesuit schools there, then in Florence and Rome. In 1577 he went to Portugal, studied the language, and a year later set out for the Portuguese colony of Goa, where he studied theology while teaching Latin and Greek. Two years later he was ordained and in 1583 entered China through Macao to found the first Catholic mission. He remained in China until his death in 1610, and very few missionaries before or since have learned as much about the culture of the peoples they sought to convert. Ricci's command of spoken Chinese was excellent, matched only by his skill in reading and in writing the classical language. He wrote literary essays which, from the standpoint of classical learning, stylistic elegance, and historical scholarship, were virtually indistinguishable from the essays written by the most prominent Chinese scholars and officials of the day.

Ricci's journals were gathered together and published posthumously in 1620, with editions in Latin, Italian, German, French, and Spanish.[39] The journals show his significant understanding and appreciation of Chinese customs, rituals, and traditions, and argue for the compatibility of these elements of Chinese civilization with the basic beliefs and practices of Christianity. He excoriated popular Buddhism and Daoism, but cultivated the Confucian literati, believing them to be convertible to the true faith, and he believed this because he also believed the classical texts revered by the Confucians could be shown to express ideas fully consonant with Christian doctrine.

More pointedly, Ricci also saw—and the later history of China was to show the clarity of his vision—that those classical texts were at the heart of a three-millennia-old cultural tradition, which was not about to be abandoned by intelligent Chinese just because it was denounced by Christian missionaries, no matter how scientifically knowledgeable or courageous or pious those missionaries might be. As a consequence, Ricci advocated what came to be called the "accommodationist" position with respect to the conversion of the Chinese: tolerance for their ancient writings, their ritual observances, and practice of ancestor worship, incorporating all of these into the Christian faith in China.

Although Ricci died before Leibniz was born, the latter's admiration for the scholarly Jesuit is clear in Leibniz's China writings, and it is Ricci's accommodationist position that Leibniz defends and advances therein. Opposed to this position was Father Nicholas Longobardi (Nicolo Longobardo, 1565–1655), who succeeded Ricci as the head of the China Mission. Longobardi believed that the ancient Chinese were materialists, and the moderns atheists, hence conversion to Christianity would require the wholesale renunciation of traditional (largely Confucian) beliefs. Unlike his predecessor, Longobardi did not cultivate the Chinese literati to any significant extent, believing that the basic tenets of Confucianism—to which all educated Chinese paid at least minimal homage—were flatly incompatible with Christian doctrine.

Longobardi set down his views in *De Confucio Ejusque Doctrina Tractatus,* written between 1622 and 1625. It was later condemned to be burned, when the Riccian position was temporarily in the ascendancy at Rome. The Dominican Fernandez Navarette, however, translated the Longobardi Latin manuscript into Spanish in 1676 to 1679 and published it. A French translation of the Spanish text was published in Paris in 1701 under the title *Traité sur quelques points de la religion des Chinois.* This French text—hereafter referred to as the *Religion Treatise*[40]—was one of the books Rémond sent to Leibniz, and much of the *Discourse* is devoted to criticizing Longobardi's views.

Longobardi was one of the relatively few Jesuits who disagreed with Ricci on the consonance of Christian and Chinese beliefs (they agreed on many other issues, however; Ricci appointed Longobardi his successor at the Mission). But most of the missionaries from other Catholic orders attacked the accommodationist position, for political if not for philosophical or theological reasons. Prominent among them was the Spanish Antonio Caballero, known also as Antonio Caballero a Santa Maria, or, as Leibniz referred to him, Antoine de Sainte-Marie.[41] This Franciscan, born in 1602, first went to China from the Spanish mission in Manila in 1633, and left three years later to take the anti-Ricci claims back to Rome. He returned to China in 1649, and remained there until he died in Guangzhou (Canton) in 1669. Shortly before his death he wrote about the Chinese Mission, but the Spanish manuscript was not published. The French translation of the text was entitled *Traité sur quelques points importants de la Mission de la Chine* (hereafter the *Mission Treatise*).[42] Published in 1701, it was the other text apparently sent to Leibniz by Rémond.[43]

Like Longobardi, Sainte-Marie believed the ancient Chinese to be materialistic (and superstitious) and their successors devoid of spiritual thoughts; hence he, too, advocated the total renunciation of China's cultural tradition as a necessary condition for Christian conversion. Thus Leibniz was no less critical of Sainte-Marie's writings than of Longobardi's, as is clearly shown in the *Remarks* and in the *Discourse*.

Among the contemporaries of Longobardi and Sainte-Marie who were more sympathetic to Ricci was Martino Martini, S.J. (1614–1661). After studying in the Collegium Romanum—Kircher was his tutor in mathematics—he went to China in 1643, the year before the final collapse of the Ming Dynasty. In 1650 he returned to Europe seeking support for the China Mission, and to present the accommodationist position at Rome. At the latter task he was successful, securing a pro-Jesuit papal decree from Alexander VII. He returned to China in 1659 and died in Hangzhou two years later.[44]

Martini wrote several works on China, the most significant of which was *Sinicae historiae decas prima. Res a gentis origine ad Christum natum in extrema Asia,* published in 1658.[45] Largely a work on Chinese history, it contained a fairly accurate chronology of early imperial reigns as the Chinese had established them. Some of the earliest reigns were seen by some Chinese (and virtually all modern scholars) as legendary, but Martini accepted them as fact. The chronology begins with Fuxi in 2952 BCE, which was troubling to many readers of Martini's work, because James Ussher's Biblical chronology had been published only a few years before and had persuaded many that creation had taken place in 4004 BCE, and the Noachian flood in 2349 BCE.[46] But if Fuxi had truly reigned over six hundred years earlier, and there were no breaks of succession to the throne, then Noah could not be the universal patriarch.

The *Sinicae historiae* also provides what was probably the first depiction in a European book of the sixty-four hexagrams of the *Yi Jing,* or *Book of Changes,* with which Leibniz was intrigued throughout his mature study of things sinological. Martini credits Fuxi with the bringing of the hexagrams to the Chinese people, and with the creation of the Chinese script based on them. (For more on the *Book of Changes,* see pp. 20 ff. below.)

The last of the writings on China which exerted a strong influence on Leibniz were those authored by the French Jesuit missionary Joachim Bouvet (1656–1730).[47] Like Verbiest, Bouvet had access to the throne, being a tutor of the Kang Xi Emperor's children. He first entered China in 1688 and remained for nine years, returning to Europe in 1697 to raise support (money, scientific equipment, and more missionaries) for the China Mission. He had read the first edition of *Novissima Sinica,* and sent Leibniz a copy of his recently published *Portrait historique de l'Empereur de la Chine.* Leibniz published parts of the *Portrait historique*—and a portrait of the Kang Xi Emperor—in the second edition of *Novissima Sinica.*[48] The correspondence between the two continued for several years after the Jesuit returned to China in 1698, the most significant exchanges taking place between 1700 and 1703.[49]

Bouvet thought on a grand scale, much more a metaphysician than historian or philologist. He conveyed many original (and sometimes far-fetched) ideas about Chinese history, language, and religion to Leibniz, based on the Figurist orientation of some Jesuits, which attempted to tease Christian figures out of non-European (i.e., pagan) writings.[50] One of these ideas was that the legendary early Chinese ruler Fuxi was not really Chinese, but a manifestation of the "Lawgiver," akin to Hermes Trismegistus in the West; indeed, on the basis of some dubious etymologies and arguments Bouvet even tried to show that Fuxi and Hermes Trismegistus were one and the same,[51] thus circumventing the creation chronology problem raised earlier by Martini's work.

Bouvet further believed that by producing the eight basic trigrams of the *Book of Changes*—which, doubled, are the sixty-four hexagrams—Fuxi had provided a notation for experiment and observation in all of the sciences. These trigrams are made up of combinations of solid and broken lines, but their mathematical and scientific significance had been, according to Bouvet, lost on later Chinese, who simply read the trigrams and hexagrams as part of a system of prognostication. More significant, after learning of Leibniz's work in binary arithmetic, Bouvet established a correlation between Leibniz's notations (0 and 1) and the broken and solid lines of Fuxi's trigrams. The philosopher's excitement upon reading Bouvet's letter describing this correspondence can easily be imagined; it is clearly discernible in the *Remarks:*

Fohi [Fuxi], the most ancient prince and philosopher of the Chinese, had understood the origin of things from unity and nothing, i.e., his mysterious figures reveal something of an analogy to Creation, containing the binary arithmetic (and yet hinting at greater things) that I rediscovered after so many thousands of years, where all numbers are written by only two notations, 0 and 1.[52]

This is a most incisive quote for understanding key elements of Leibniz's thought. In the first place, by saying "rediscovered," he links himself to a significant extent with a certain tradition of Christian apologetics that began at least as early as Lactantius (fl. ca. 300 CE). Sometimes referred to as the "Ancient Theology,"[53] this apologetic strain relied on texts, or fragments of texts, attributed to such authors as Pythagoras, Hermes Trismegistus, Orpheus, and others, and claimed to find fundamental tenets of Christianity prefigured in those texts. But in order not to challenge Biblical revelation, ancient theologies attributed the original ideas found in these works either to Moses, Noah, or Enoch. While Leibniz nowhere commits himself fully to the view that Hermetic writings precede the time of Christ, he nevertheless takes seriously the arguments of the ancient theologians, which he usually refers to as "early Church Fathers."[54]

A second insight into Leibniz's views contained in this quote comes from the parenthetical remark: "and yet hinting at greater things." Earlier in 1697 he had written a letter to Duke Rudolph August,[55] which included the design of a medallion he wished to be struck. The obverse is merely a portrait of the Duke, but the reverse gives binary equivalents for several Arabic numerals, under which he inscribed *Imago Creationis*. He also portrays rays of light shining down into the watery deep, and equates the latter with Zero and the former with "the almighty One."

Leibniz never sent this letter, but he does seem to be sincere in believing that his binary arithmetic was theologically as well as scientifically important, capable of unlocking secrets both of nature and the Book of Genesis, and generating all the natural numbers using only 0 and 1, symbolizing in a most dramatic way the *creatio ex nihilo* by the one God. In another letter to Bouvet (18 May 1703), responding to the Jesuit's linking of the eight trigrams with the numbers 0 to 7, Leibniz says:

. . . the last is the most perfect and the Sabbath, for in it everything has been made and fulfilled; thus 7 is written 111 without 0 . . .[56]

Thus, knowledge of China could only increase Leibniz's sympathies for the "Ancient Theology" in one form or another, all the more so as he knew of early Roman contacts with China and had read of the Jesuit "discovery" in Xian of a stele inscribed in both Syriac and Chinese, concrete evidence of Nestorian penetration of China early in the Christian era. Kircher published the inscriptions in 1667, and while many Europeans doubted their authenticity, Leibniz (correctly) did not, as he makes clear in his *Preface*.[57]

Hence, on the basis of Bouvet's claim that the Chinese of 4,500 years ago possessed a mathematical notation similar to his own—which was useful for the exemplification of both reason and revelation—Leibniz not only found support for the accommodationist position, but he was also able to believe, thanks to his faith in reason, that the conversion of the Chinese could proceed apace once it was demonstrated to them that later generations had simply lost the true meaning of Fuxi's work.

In sum, Leibniz's knowledge of China, especially Chinese thought, came primarily from men who saw the country, its peoples and its culture through the filter of their own. For most of them—the missionaries—this situation was exacerbated by their avowed purpose in going to China: to Christianize it. But their manifold biases notwithstanding, these missionaries learned much of China, and those who advocated toleration and moderation—especially Ricci, Verbiest, Martini, Grimaldi, and Bouvet—came not only to have an appreciation of the Chinese heritage that was uncommon among Europeans, but to transmit their appreciation to Leibniz as well.[58] Both the accommodationists and their opponents were the initiators of sinological studies in the West, guaranteeing that they would have biases and make mistakes even without the handicap of bringing a strong Christian perspective to bear on the decidedly non-Christian culture they were studying, or engaging in political and theological disputes. If those biases and mistakes are now easily seen, the ease is due in no small measure to the growth of scholarship that followed the initial missionary cultivation of the field.

III. *The Chinese Intellectual Tradition*

Leibniz's substantive writings on China, especially on Chinese beliefs, were never undertaken solely to explicate, analyze, and evaluate those beliefs. Rather were they composed largely to rebut the claims of the anti-accommodationists that the Chinese were truly heathen and must therefore forswear their cultural heritage in order to become good (European-like) Christians.

The rebuttal rests of course on Leibniz's own philosophical ideas, but, equally important, also on his own views of Chinese intellectual history, which caused him to distinguish sharply among and between the ideas of the ancient Chinese, and the Chinese encountered by the missionaries. In order to place the manifold temporal references in his writings in their proper context, it is thus necessary to outline the order of development of Chinese thought and Leibniz's views thereof.

For purposes of understanding the arguments in Leibniz's China writings, the history—real and legendary—of Chinese thought must be divided into three discontinuous ages: (1) the era of the sage kings, from the twenty-ninth through the twelfth centuries BCE; (2) the period of Confucius and his classical successors, from the sixth through the third centuries BCE; and (3) the "modern" period of Neo-Confucianism, with its criticisms of Buddhism, beginning in the eleventh century CE and continuing to Leibniz's own day.[59]

The Methuselah-like reigns attributed to them suggest that the earliest legendary rulers of China were just that: legendary. There is no evidence—except for the legends, written millennia later—that China was a major civilization circa 3000 BCE, the time period in which Leibniz (via Bouvet and others) placed Fuxi and the oldest strata of the *Yi Jing.*

The earliest date in Chinese recorded history confirmed by archaeological work is the sixteenth century BCE, the period of the Shang Dynasty, whose traditional dates are 1766–1050 BCE. The artifacts recovered from Shang sites reveal highly sophisticated technological and artistic abilities in such areas as architecture, bronze casting, and writing, which show that Chinese civilization, as a civilization, must go back to at least the nineteenth or eighteenth centuries BCE; but this is still more than a thousand years later than the dates accepted by Leibniz.[60]

Moreover, it bears emphasizing that there are no Chinese texts which can be shown to be earlier than approximately the eleventh century BCE, and even these documents are fragmentary and/or contain much material that was interpolated many centuries later. Thus, although the missionaries and Leibniz refer to the sage kings as China's "most ancient philosophers," there are not even fragments of philosophical writings that can be attributed to them with any scholarly confidence.

In attempting to understand Leibniz's views of China, however, the historicity of the legendary rulers is perhaps less important than the qualities the legends attribute to them. In addition to Fuxi, Leibniz mentions the emperors Yao, Shun, and others, who share similar characteristics. First, they were not supernaturally endowed; they lived to very ripe old ages, but all eventually died, and during their lifetimes performed no feats that contravened the laws of physics. Second, the sage kings were highly intelligent, and they put their intelligence to good use in the service of the Chinese people by their inventions and discoveries (medicine, agriculture, irrigation, writing, and so forth). And third, the sage kings were moral exemplars, endeavoring to rule by moral suasion rather than force. From his writings it is apparent that Leibniz was aware of these qualities, and he uses the morality and intelligence accorded them— especially Fuxi—in making his case for the religiosity of the ancient Chinese. Indeed, his highest praise for Chinese thinkers is given to these men.

After the period of the sage kings, the next significant time period referred to by Leibniz (not always clearly) begins many centuries later, with the birth of Confucius (551–479 BCE). No philosophical works prior to his time (if, indeed, any were written) have survived, and there is little evidence that any were extant during his lifetime. Works on other topics were produced, however, and several of them have come down to the present: books of poetry, governmental records, history, rituals, divination, and so forth. Some of these works received special attention from Confucius and his followers, who read philosophical and religious themes into them. These books became classics (*jing*), and like the *Iliad* and *Odyssey* in Greece, were not only a basic part of, but came to define the later cultural tradition of the Chinese. Three of these classics are cited specifically by Leibniz in his writings, and thereby deserve specific mention.

1. The Yi Jing (易 經), or Book of Changes[61]

This book has several components, not all of which were written at the same time. The oldest strata are divinatory in nature: symbolic descriptions of the sixty-four hexagrams which comprise the basic text. According to the *Yi Jing,* change takes place in the universe because of the complementary interaction of two fundamental principles, the *yin* (陰) and the *yang*

(陽). *Yin* denotes passivity, receptivity, and descent, and represents the female principle, a mare, the earth, darkness, valleys, and the mother. The *yang* principle is active and ascending, male, light, heaven, mountains, a dragon, and the father. In the *Yi Jing* the female principle is symbolized by a broken line (– –), and the male principle by a solid one (—).

By means of a formulaic counting out of yarrow (milfoil) stalks, a person consults the oracle, obtaining at the end of the count either a *yin* or a *yang* number, which is recorded as a broken or unbroken line. The counting ritual is repeated six times, until a hexagram (six lines) is obtained, and the several female and/or male lines which make up the hexagram represent, in symbolic form, the diviner's place in the universe at the time of consultation.

The hexagrams probably grew out of an earlier symbolic tradition of trigrams[62] (three lines), which represented familial, social, and natural phenomena. Thus, three consecutive *yang* lines (☰) represented South, heaven, the head, and the father, while three *yin* lines (☷) stood for North, earth, the abdomen, mother, and so forth. One *yang* line followed by two *yin* (☳) stood for thunder, etc., and the oldest son; one *yin* line between two *yang* (☲) represented lightning, East . . . , and the middle daughter. Hence the hexagrams, read on the one hand as the sum of six lines, and on the other as being made up of two trigrams, were replete with a metaphorical symbolism sufficiently rich that a good deal of concentration and meditation was necessary on the part of the diviner in order to determine the significance of the hexagram obtained.

As a consequence, the *Yi Jing* must not be seen simplistically as a fortune-telling manual; no medium is needed to interpret the symbols, and the motive for consultation is not so much to predict the future as it is to orient oneself properly in the natural and social order of things. Nor should the *Yi* be read as a proto-scientific work, in the sense that the term *science* is used today. It bears repeating that the *yin* and *yang* principles were seen by the Chinese as complementary rather than as antagonistic, and that these symbolized principles were not so much empirical explanations as they were metaphorical constructs. As an illustration, a non-Chinese would probably symbolize peace, or stability—using the *Yi Jing* paraphernalia— as ☶☷; that is, heaven above and earth below. But remember that *yang* rises while *yin* descends, so that stability would be enhanced by having heaven below and earth above: ☷☰—the *Yi Jing* hexagram for "Peace"; the former hexagram is "Splitting Apart."[63]

The Chinese tradition—passed on to Leibniz through Bouvet and others—attributes the formation of the eight basic trigrams to Fuxi, circa 2900 BCE. More probably the oldest strata of the text date from about 1100–1000 BCE at the earliest. In addition to the trigrams, hexagrams, and their descriptions, the *Book of Changes* also contains commentaries on them, and on the individual lines of some hexagrams. These commentaries were written much later, perhaps as late as the third century BCE, and are much more philosophical in nature than the earlier strata, without, however, altering the basically contemplative quality of the book as a whole.

In writing about the *Yi Jing* to Leibniz, Bouvet (and others) dismissed the symbolic and divinatory elements of the work, focusing instead on the sequence of broken and unbroken lines. For Bouvet[64] these lines could be read in the first place as isomorphic with Leibniz's system of binary arithmetical notation, with 0 represented by – –, and 1 by —. Thus all of Leibniz's translations of numbers from base 10 to base 2 notation were similarly translatable into the *Yi Jing* notation of *yin* and *yang* lines. There is a way of ordering the hexagrams so that they can be read, using the Leibniz–Bouvet isomorphism, as an arithmetical progression from 0 to 63.[65]

But Bouvet read even more into the trigrams: he saw them as the oldest form of Chinese writing, and, because he saw some similarities between the trigrams and ancient Hebrew (his correspondence does not say what those similarities are), he assumed that in the very ancient past the Chinese had received the culture of the West.[66] Many of Bouvet's ideas would not be given much credence today, but it might be noted that his view of the trigrams as being the first Chinese writing does have some traditional support.[67] The tradition rests on the fact that a few Chinese characters bear a resemblance to certain trigrams (and hexagrams). The most striking example is the character for water 水, which was anciently written 川. Turned horizontally with its lines straightened, this would look like ☵, which is the trigram symbolizing (running) water in the *Book of Changes*.

2. *The Shu Jing* 書經 [68]

Translated as the *Book of History*, or the *Book of Documents*, parts of the *Shu Jing* may be China's oldest written work, dating from the eleventh century

BCE. It is made up of a series of small essays, memorials, and documents which record parts of reigns of the sage-kings Yao, Shun, Yu, the reigns of several Xia Dynasty rulers (traditional dates 2205–1766 BCE), Shang rulers after them, and the early years of the Zhou Dynasty (1050–256 BCE) under Kings Wen, Wu, the Duke of Zhou, and their successors. It is by no means a complete history of antiquity, and the oldest parts of it were written down long after the events described therein were supposed to have occurred. Further, several sections of the *Shu Jing* were interpolated into the text at a later date, some of them undoubtedly after the time of Confucius.

Although parts of the *Shu* are simply chronicles of events, other parts of it are the charges of rulers to their successors, or to their subordinate ministers, and the themes repeated in those exhortations had political and moral qualities that came to be definitive of the ideal Confucian state. Those in positions of authority were commanded to: *a*) work for the welfare of the people; *b*) maintain the rites and ritual observances of their ancestors; *c*) be frugal; *d*) view their position as a trust conferred by Heaven (*tian* 天), which was not so much a symbol of deity as it was a reflection of the natural order; *e*) obtain and keep harmony within the social order, and between the social and natural order. Many of the practices and ritual observances described in the *Shu Jing* were surely based on early beliefs in the supernatural, but these beliefs are not emphasized in the book, and were virtually ignored by Confucius and his followers during the classical period.

3. The Shi Jing (Book of Poetry, Book of Odes, or Book of Songs)[69]
詩 經

According to the disciples of Confucius, he regularly quoted lines from the *Shi Jing* to emphasize an ethical, aesthetic, social, or political point he wanted to make. The original 314 poems which make up the book, however, are just that: poems. While some of them do indeed have morals that can easily be read out of them, the majority of them are simply reflective of early Chinese life. There are love poems, and poems lamenting a son or husband going off to war; poems dealing with nature; with hunting and fishing; with friendship; with festivals; and there are poems dealing with legends and ancient rituals. Together the poems of the *Shi*

Jing paint what must be the most accurate picture we have of the everyday life of a Chinese living in approximately the ninth century BCE.

Returning to Confucius, he would probably have been surprised to learn that the "Period of the Philosophers" in China is dated from his birth. He said of himself that he was a transmitter rather than an innovator,[70] i.e., a classicist rather than a philosopher. This autobiographical statement is not entirely accurate—Confucius was an original thinker by any standard—but the statement does capture an essential ingredient of Confucianism: a deep respect and affection for the rich cultural heritage of the past. He saw the ideal state as having existed during the reigns of the ancient sage kings and advocated a return to their principles of government. According to Confucius (and the *Shu, Shi,* and other early works), the sage kings governed on the basis of ritual and custom rather than law or force, were themselves reverent toward the past, were more concerned to insure the material and spiritual well-being of the people than in accumulating personal wealth, and saw as their main task the maintenance of harmony between the collective society and the natural order, as noted above.

Like many other epochal thinkers of the ancient world, Confucius never wrote anything that has survived. All that we know of his views with assurance comes from the *Lun Yu* (論 語) often translated as the *Analects;* Leibniz refers to it as the *"Lung Yu," "Lun Iu," "Lun Ju",* and the *"Su Lum Iu."* The bulk of the book is a collection of very brief conversations between the Master and his disciples, but parts of the work may have been written down a full century or so after Confucius died. Many other writings have been attributed to him, and he is supposed to have edited some of the classics; but it is now widely held (as it was not during Leibniz's day) that the only solid text for ascertaining the Master's views is the *Lun Yu.*[71]

Most Western interpreters of Confucius, and not a few modern Chinese themselves, portray China's First Teacher as a thoroughgoing rationalist, agnostic in religious matters if not downright atheistic. There is some textual evidence for this view, which is not too enthusiastically cited by Leibniz in his writings, especially in the *Discourse.* Such a portrayal, however, can be overdrawn; the "this-worldliness" of Confucius notwithstanding, there are also significant passages in the *Lun Yu* which show that he was at times greatly concerned with what would today be considered non- or ir-rational matters. Thus, he is supposed to have lamented that "Heaven had forsaken him" in one passage, believed that Heaven had given him a special mission in another, and in still others he was troubled by the fact that neither in his dreams nor his observations of natural phenomena had he been given a "sign" that he would be successful in his efforts.[72]

Such seemingly other-worldly concerns, however, were not the kind Leibniz sought in seeking comparisons with Christian doctrine. Interpreters of Confucius may never agree on the extent to which he focused on the secular over the sacred, or the magical, but they all agree that he was neither a metaphysician nor a theologian in the Western sense of those terms. The *Lun Yu* discusses ethics, rituals, customs, sociopolitical issues, and aesthetics in some detail, but there are no discussions of first principles, God, primary or secondary matter, reason, and so forth; there are no discussions, in other words, of the major concepts Leibniz discusses in his writings. It is for this reason that Leibniz refers somewhat less to Confucius himself than to his legendary predecessors, or later followers, the descriptions of whom can be more easily read as having Christian and/or cosmological implications, at least by stalwart readers.

The most famous successor to Confucius was Mencius, who lived one hundred and fifty years later (ca. 372–289 BCE). In the book 孟子 that bears his name,[73] Mencius elaborated the views of Confucius, and while he did discuss some of the concepts taken up by Leibniz, for the most part the "Second Sage" of Confucianism shared the nonmetaphysical and nontheological perspective of his predecessor.

Not until the *Li Ji* (禮 記), or *Records of Ritual*,[74] do we find a Confucian text that begins to link ethics and socio-political thought with cosmological speculation (and even in this book the speculations are not lengthy). The *Li Ji* was probably made up in its present form during the second century BCE, and the forty-nine heterogeneous chapters which comprise it treat topics ranging from the details of social etiquette to cosmology. The book is fundamentally concerned with customs, rituals, duties, and manners; one can find in it the proper form of address to one's in-laws, sacrifices to be made by the emperor, detailed instructions for bathing one's parents, and so forth. Some of the chapters, however, attempt to link these ceremonial duties with the place of human beings in the universe, and two of these chapters (39 and 28) were singled out centuries later as worthy of especial study: the *Da Xue* (大 學), or *Great Learning,* and the *Jung Yung* (中 庸), or *Doctrine of the Mean.* The latter work is quoted several times by Leibniz in the *Discourse,* as coming from

Confucius; almost surely it was written by some disciple(s) of his disciples, but it is an authentic early Confucian work. In any event, these two short works, together with the *Mencius* and *Lun Yu*, are the "Four Books" to which Leibniz also makes reference in his writings.[75] Taken together, these four texts can be read a variety of ways, but their basic thrust is clear and can be summarized succinctly by the lines from Pope: "Presume then not God to scan // the proper study of mankind is man."

In summary, while classical Confucianism is correctly characterized as religious and philosophical, the religion deals much more with immanence than transcendence, and the philosophy is ethical, aesthetic, and sociopolitical. The very early ritual practices (of the Shang and early Zhou) inherited by Confucius and his followers were originally derived from supernatural beliefs, but those beliefs, while never explicitly repudiated, were nevertheless not widely discussed or debated among the educated during the period in which he lived. The *Lun Yu* records, for example, that when a disciple asked the Master whether the spirits of the ancestors were present during the ritual sacrifices to them, he replied, "As yet you know so little about life; why do you ask about death?"[76]

In other words, Confucius saw clearly that those ritual links with a rich cultural past were too important to be lost in a more skeptical age, no matter what the original inspiration for those practices may have been (surely one does not have to be a Christian to be moved by a Bach cantata). Thus he devoted his energies, as did those who followed him, to preserving those cultural links by placing them in a social and humanistic context.[77] With their steady focus on tradition, customs, rituals, and rites, the early Confucians laid claim to being the guardians and transmitters of the Chinese heritage. It is for this reason that, ever since the classical period, referring to a person as a Confucian often meant little more than that he was a typical member of the literati.

The third period of Chinese intellectual history significant for Leibniz begins over a thousand years later. After many centuries of being eclipsed by the Buddhism imported from India, the Confucian classical texts underwent a thorough reexamination in the light of the changes in Chinese thought brought about by Buddhist doctrines and by the changes in political and cultural patterns that accompanied China's growth as an empire. This reexamination marked the beginning of what has come to be called Neo-Confucianism, and many of the philosophers mentioned by Leibniz in his China writings were formative of the renewal of the classical tradition: Zhang Cai (1020–1077), the Cheng brothers,[78] and especially the encyclopedic Zhu Xi (1130–1200).[79] Taking some passages from the *Yi Jing*, from the *Mencius, Jung Yung*, and from other classical texts, the Neo-Confucians constructed a metaphysical system in which to place the older Confucian concerns with moral, social, and political questions. Where the classical Confucians discussed primary obligations, the Neo-Confucians discussed primary principles; earlier critiques of benevolence and righteousness were later followed by critiques of "ether" and "matter"; and whereas the classical texts placed great emphasis on describing the details of ritual sacrifices, the Neo-Confucians described to whom and why the sacrifices were being made. This is not to suggest that the Neo-Confucians distorted fundamentally the views or writings of their forerunners. On the contrary, they used their metaphysics to justify the earlier Confucian way of life: spiritual advancement could not proceed without fulfilling one's many obligations to family and society.

Put another way, the Neo-Confucians did not—by their lights—break with their classical predecessors. Rather, against an intellectual background strongly permeated by abstract Buddhist metaphysics, they attempted to provide metaphysical underpinnings for the views of their early heroes. One of the central threads which ties the earlier and the later Confucians together is the importance of self-cultivation, not only for aesthetic development and moral strength, but for spiritual insight as well. The discipline involved in self-cultivation takes on a contemplative element in Neo-Confucianism that is largely absent in the classical tradition, but the emphasis on self-cultivation and personal discipline is constant. The secular can become sacred.[80]

To see the secular as sacred would not be difficult for, say, a Zuni or an Akan, but would probably strain the vision of the average adherent of the Abrahamic religions, hence Leibniz should not be significantly faulted for not apprehending this basic feature of the Confucian persuasion, or seeing that it linked the early Confucians closely with their ethical and spiritual descendants. (Of course, none of Leibniz's anti-accommodationist opponents saw Confucianism in this way either.)

Neo-Confucianism came to dominate Chinese intellectual life until the twentieth century. By the time of the Ming Dynasty (1368–1644), the history and philosophy of China as interpreted by Zhu Xi became required reading for everyone, the Chinese examination system being based on Zhu's writings and commentaries on the classics. In 1422 a major compendium of classical texts and early commentaries, with later commentaries by Zhu Xi and many other Neo-Confucians, was compiled. It was called the *Xingli Da Chuan Shu* (性 理 大 全 書), hereafter cited as the *Compendium*,[81] and is the Chinese source most often quoted by Leibniz, as it was by the missionaries Longobardi and Ste.-Marie.[82] The form of the *Compendium* is partially responsible for the fact that at times Leibniz attributes views to philosophers of the ancient period which were actually the views of the Neo-Confucians. The anthology contains materials that span 23 centuries, and neither Longobardi nor Ste.-Marie, who quote at length from the *Compendium*, always make clear whether they are citing passages from a classical text or from a commentary thereon. Indeed, parts of the *Religion Treatise* and the *Mission Treatise* suggest that even the two missionaries are not always sure whom, or what, they are quoting; this is especially true for Longobardi, who erroneously attributes much of the compilation of the *Compendium* to scholars of the tenth century BCE.[83]

The resurgence of Confucianism did not, of course, lead to the demise of Buddhism, nor of Daoism, the second major philosophical and religious tradition indigenous to China. In Chinese religion, however, the several belief systems were not as sharply demarcated, nor were they as exclusive as Western religious groupings have tended to be. Depending on the locale, the common people adopted different but equally rich and complex admixtures of beliefs, rituals, heroes, heroines, and deities drawn from local history and legend, Confucianism, Daoism, and Buddhism; sufficiently rich and complex that sorting out the distinguishing features of each source was (and continues to be) a difficult task.

Moreover, by the time Father Ricci arrived in China to found the first Christian mission, there was a fairly strong and well-developed syncretic movement among the intelligentsia, with many efforts being made philosophically to merge the "Three Schools into One." This movement can be traced to the Song period (960–1279) and grew during the early Ming. It has been argued that many emperors endorsed the syncretism as a means of increasing their power and social control.[84] This helps to explain why many later Ming and Qing (1644–1911) Neo-Confucians struggled to keep their belief system free of the "impurities" of Daoism and Buddhism.[85]

Ming and Qing Neo-Confucians faced another fundamental problem. With the passage of time, the examination system for entrance into the civil service became ever more formalized, and thus, not surprisingly, fossilized. Preparing and sitting for the examinations required great physical stamina, much rote memorization, and mind- and soul-numbing attentiveness to minutiae; none of which is generally conducive to self-cultivation or spiritual insight. As a consequence, many highly intelligent and deeply sensitive scholars either failed the examinations repeatedly or refused to sit for them. At the same time, however, no concerted outcry against the examination system could be forthcoming from these Confucians, for it was the major barrier preventing eunuchs, military officers, merchants, and other (as the Confucians saw it) cutpurses, footpads, and related self-seeking ne'er-do-wells from entering the civil service; which would destroy the civilization they (the Confucians) were dedicated to preserving and enhancing.[86]

Seen in this light, it should not be surprising that by the time the Christian missionaries got their bearings in China there were many members of the intelligentsia who were, if not nihilists, then certainly of a somewhat cynical turn of mind. They followed the official state, clan, and familial ritual observances prescribed by custom and the Classics, but otherwise did not emphasize spiritual self-cultivation, or personal discipline, or even accept the metaphysical pronouncements of the earlier Neo-Confucians. It is significantly due to meeting a number of such men that anti-accommodationists like Longobardi and Sainte-Marie concluded that the Chinese had to abandon completely their Chinese ways of thinking if they were to become true Christians. Leibniz did not hold such "Confucians" in very high regard, made clear by the epithets—"Modern Atheists," "Skeptics," and "Hypocrites"—by which he referred to them in his writings.

In summary, it is essential to appreciate the peculiar role played by Confucianism in shaping Chinese thought, culture, and daily life as well. As a philosophy, with religious overtones, Confucianism was the dominant belief system among the literate for most of the last two millennia. And because governmental officials were drawn from the ranks of the literate, Confucianism came to be the official state ideology as well as the major intellectual force in China, largely unchallenged despite political problems that stemmed from its "official" status. Moreover, because Confucianism celebrated tradition, with all its rituals, familial obligations, ancestor worship, and so forth, it was exemplified in the lives of most traditional Chinese commoners, who were thereby Confucians by practice even though they had no firsthand acquaintance with the philosophical or the traditional texts. Confucius, then, was not simply one philosopher among many; his defense and enhancement of the early Chinese heritage caused him to be seen as the symbol of Chinese civilization, and he was consequently revered even by those whose views were different (Daoists and Buddhists), and by those who could not read the writings which contained those views (the common people). Thus, the spirit of Confucianism was reflected strongly in the writings and actions of Confucian philosophers, and in addition, it thoroughly permeated the entire fabric of Chinese culture.

Although Leibniz occasionally attributes a correct Confucian view to the wrong Confucian, and at other times attributes views to them which no Confucian held, he did appreciate deeply the significance of the Confucian tradition in China. Like Father Ricci before him, Leibniz also appreciated that no other belief system would have an impact in that country unless it came to terms with the country's intellectual heritage. It was for this reason that he wrote on Chinese thought, attempting to pour some Christian wine in Confucian and pre-Confucian bottles.

IV. *The Texts and their Translations*

1. *Preface to the Novissima Sinica*

The textual situation concerning Leibniz's *Preface* is a complicated one. An original draft is at the Lower Saxony State Library: *Briefwechsel* 306, fol. 21–24; but no fair copy is extant. The first printed edition appeared in 1697, and a second—which included the Bouvet materials—in 1699. (Neither edition gives a publisher or place of publication.)

Differences between the two printed editions are minor, and the original draft at times differs from both. Leibniz made many changes in his draft, and may well have written another manuscript, and/or corrected the galley proofs of the printed editions; but such corrected texts do not appear to exist.

The best printed edition of the original Latin is in H-G. Nesselrath and H. Reinbothe, *Das Neueste von China* (1697): *Novissima Sinica*,[87] which contains a German translation of the *Preface* as well as of many other materials from the book itself. They footnote all of the variants between the draft and the printed editions, but their actual transcription of the text incorporates only some of them.

There are two complete French translations of the *Preface:* Paul Bornet, S.J., "La Préface des Novissima Sinica,"[88] and Christiane Frémont, "Préface des Dernières nouvelles de la Chine"[89].

The benchmark of scholarship on this text is Donald F. Lach's *The Preface to Leibniz's Novissima Sinica*, now long out of print.[90] After going through the original draft (unavailable to Lach) and printed editions of the *Preface*, including the German and French translations and commentaries on it, and then comparing the work to Lach's, we found little—either in his translation, textual notes, or commentary—to improve upon. All of the changes we wished to make were sufficiently minor that we thought it proper—and a fitting tribute to a distinguished senior colleague—to simply request his permission (and that of the University of Hawaii Press) to reproduce his translation of the *Preface* for the present volume, which was graciously given.

We have made alterations to Lach's rendering of the Latin text in §4, §7, §11, §13, §15, §17, §18, §20, and §21. Because our introductory materials differ from his in scope and content, and because other texts of Leibniz are cross-referenced herein, we have also altered and reduced Lach's footnotes to his translation, and added a number of our own. All of our notes which more or less parallel Lach's conclude with a reference to his notes and/or his splendid Introduction to the text. The only other change we have made, for purposes of uniformity in the several translations, is to replace Lach's Roman numerals numbering Leibniz's paragraphs with Arabic numerals.

2. The Civil Cult of Confucius

The translation is based on Leibniz's draft of an addition he appended to a letter sent to the Jesuit Antoine Verjus in Paris. It is found in *Briefwechsel* 954, fol. 32–33. A copy, corrected in Leibniz's hand, probably dates from the following year, and is in *Briefwechsel* 274, fol. 6–7.

The best printed edition of Leibniz's autograph is in Rita Widmaier, *Leibniz Korrespondiert mit China*[91] (which does not contain a German translation; Widmaier has made one, however, and kindly shared it with us). Another printed edition is in I. Klutstein-Rojtman and Zwi Werblosky, "Leibniz: De cultu Confucii civili," which also includes an excellent French translation of the text.[92]

Leibniz dated the letter New Year's Day, 1700 (according to the old Julian calendar), and Verjus acknowledged receipt of it, and *De cultu*. The copy of the letter, however, includes in the marginalia (but crossed out) a reference to *Historia cultus Sinensium*, which was published in—probably in the autumn of—1700. This book contains the 1693 decree of Charles Maigrot, Apostolic Vicar of Fujian, forbidding the use of *tian* and *shang di* as appellations for God. Leibniz seems to have known of this decree earlier, however, for there appears to be an oblique reference to it in his *Preface* §12 (see fn. 18 thereto). One commentator thus suggests *De cultu* was written as a response to the Maigrot decree.[93] However, Leibniz also criticizes Antoine Arnauld in the *Preface* (§11), and another commentator has suggested that *De cultu* was composed as a rebuttal to the latter's views on Chinese thought.[94]

The text is clearly a defense of the Riccian position, to whomever and when it was originally written. In the body of his letter to Verjus, Leibniz says he is sending him a copy of an "extract" entitled *De cultu Confucii civili*, which he had earlier addressed to a friend who is not named.

The numbering of the paragraphs in the text is our own.

3. *Remarks on Chinese Rites and Religion*

In a brief letter to Bartholomaeus des Bosses dated 12 August 1709, Leibniz says he is including some remarks he had noted down the year before about the rites and religion of the Chinese. Their correspondence had begun in 1706, and continued until shortly before Leibniz's death in 1716. Although he never went to China, des Bosses was keenly interested in things Chinese, and was an admirer of Leibniz's work, translating the latter's *Theodicy* into Latin.

The letter to des Bosses is printed in L. Dutens, *G.G. Leibnitii: Opera Omnia*,[95] but the appended remarks are not. Both are printed in C.I. Gerhardt's *Die philosophische Schriften von G.W. Leibniz*.[96] Again, the original manuscript (in Latin) is in the Lower Saxony State Library, *Briefwechsel* 95, fol. 91–92.

The present translation, based on the original manuscript and following the excellent transcription of it by Gerhardt, marks the first appearance of the *Remarks on Chinese Rites and Religion* in English. We have also consulted the French translation by Christiane Frémont,[97] and an unpublished German translation by Rita Widmaier, who, again, very kindly made her work available to us. As with *De cultu,* we are responsible for the numbering of the paragraphs.

This text includes the first references Leibniz makes to the missionary writings of Fathers Longobardi and Sainte-Marie, and, in outline form, sketches the strategy he will follow in defending the accommodationist position with respect to the Chinese in his major work on the subject, the *Discourse on the Natural Theology of the Chinese.*

4. The Discourse on the Natural Theology of the Chinese

We published the first English translation of this text in 1977 with the University Press of Hawaii as no. 4 in the Society for Asian and Comparative Philosophy Monograph Series. It was reissued in 1980 but has been out of print for several years. Going through the text again fifteen years later, and aided by a number of helpful comments and criticisms made by reviewers of the first edition,[98] we have made a number of corrections to our original text. About the history of the text itself, however, we have found no reason to change what was said in the earlier edition, and therefore the following three paragraphs are reproduced therefrom, with only minor changes.[99]

During the later years of his life, Leibniz maintained an intensive and extensive correspondence with Nicholas Rémond. The text now known as the *Monadology* was originally a letter written to the latter in 1714, and a little over a year later Leibniz began composing the *Discourse,* addressed to the same correspondent. In a letter of 13 January 1716 to des Bosses,[100] and another to Rémond dated 27 January 1716,[101] Leibniz wrote that he had completed the work but two months later wrote to the latter again, saying, "I need more time to finish completely my discourse on the natural theology of the Chinese."[102] He never found the time, and the *Discourse* was never sent.

This translation is based on the original and only draft of Leibniz's autograph, to be found in the Lower Saxony State Library in Hannover, Germany, *Leibniz-Handschriften,* XXXVII, 1810, no. 1, entitled (by a later archivist) *Lettre de Mr. Leibniz touchant les Chinois.* No fair copy of the draft is extant, and several of the sixteen folio pages are frayed, making certain passages either illegible or incomplete. For this reason it has been necessary at times to rely on the earliest printed edition of the *Discourse,* which is found in C. Kortholt's edition of *Viri illustris Godefridi Guil. Leibnitii Epistolae ad diversos.*[103] In the same volume Kortholt also includes the *Religion Treatise* of Longobardi (pp. 165–266) and the *Mission Treatise* of Ste.-Marie (pp. 268–412)—complete with Leibniz's footnotes on them—which are the editions of the missionary texts that have been consulted and are cited herein.[104] Having the advantage of working from a fully preserved manuscript, the Kortholt edition, despite many errors of transcription, is the only source for some lacunae in Leibniz's manuscript. The later edition of Dutens (IV, 169–210) is not helpful in this regard because Dutens used the Kortholt edition (and not the original manuscript) for his printing of the text. Both Kortholt and Dutens entitled the work *Lettre de M. G.G. Leibniz sur la Philosophie Chinoise à M. de Rémond.* Kortholt himself, like many early editors of Leibniz's untitled writings, is responsible for the title, the numbering of the paragraphs, and also for the division of the manuscript into four parts and their subtitles as well. He also gave short descriptive titles (omitted from this translation) to each numbered paragraph, inserting them collectively at the beginning of each part.

Given the unsatisfactory and at times incomplete transcriptions found in both of these editions, it is fortunate that the 1968 German translation of the *Discourse* by R. Loosen and F. Vonessen includes a new printing of the French text as well.[105] Without in any way wishing to detract from their commendable scholarship, the present translation differs significantly from Loosen–Vonessen at times, both with respect to translations and to transcriptions from the original manuscript. This German edition offers the best printing of the French original at present, and the numbering of the paragraphs in our translation is taken from them; the following note lists all the variants where we found their text differing from the original.[106]

In the *Discourse* Leibniz makes numerous references to the *Mission Treatise* of Longobardi and the *Religion Treatise* of Ste.-Marie. We have made Leibniz's citations thereof uniform, with the former cited by both a section and a page number, separated by a full colon, and the latter simply by page number.

5. On General Matters Concerning Translation

The first three of the translations presented herein were written in Latin, the fourth in French. From the numerous changes he made in the extant autograph copies of all of them, it is evident that Leibniz did not consider any of them a complete or polished text. The French of the *Discourse* in particular suffers from many stylistic and orthographic inconsistencies. Consequently, except in passages deemed essential for understanding the texts, no effort has been made to be precise in the transcription of Leibniz's manuscripts in this regard. An exception is the transliteration of Chinese terms. While it would have made for a smoother and clearer reading of his writings to have standardized, in English transliteration, all of Leibniz's various spellings of the Chinese, it would have attributed to him a familiarity with those terms which he may not have had. His Chinese transliterations, therefore, have uniformly been transcribed precisely so that readers of the texts may judge for themselves when, and where, Leibniz did or did not know he was writing a variant spelling of the same term he had used in another place. To compensate for this narrative difficulty, each Chinese term (when known) has been transliterated in the standard English form in the footnotes, and all variant spellings have been similarly noted, transliterated, and cross-referenced when they appear. In addition, the Chinese original for each term mentioned by Leibniz is given on its first occurrence in the manuscripts.

Relatedly, we appreciate that nonsinologists will have a more difficult time reading these materials and referring to our sources because we have employed the *pinyin* system of transliteration of Chinese terms now standard in China, rather than the older Wade–Giles system used in most English-language translations of, and writings on, Chinese thought. By way of apology, a transcription table between the two systems of Romanization is given at the back of this book.

Leibniz's narrative inconsistencies and difficulties are not confined to Chinese terms. It is clear that he did not edit the *Discourse,* for example—a simple arithmetical error of addition is found in part IV[107]—and his French is often archaic and opaque, abounding in many lengthy and convoluted sentences. There being no point in translating vague French (and occasional Latin) sentences into confusing English ones, Leibniz's sentence structures have often been modified in these translations, largely through the use of colons and semicolons, parentheses, and dashes. In the few instances where there was an irreconcilable conflict between his French or Latin and his obvious (from the context) intent, the latter has been determinative; what distinguished Leibniz is his philosophical reasoning and not his literary abilities in non-native languages. Whenever a linguistic liberty with the texts has been taken, it has been noted; for the rest, the careful Leibniz scholar may consult either the original manuscripts or the best printed editions we have cited above.

Leibniz underlines often, but inconsistently, in his writing: sometimes to emphasize, sometimes because he is quoting, sometimes for a Chinese term. To preserve his texts, we have regularly underlined (not italicized) where he underlined; we have italicized only where it is obvious (i.e., in references to titles such as the *Novissima Sinica*) and in our own employment of Chinese terms in the notes and elsewhere.

Relatedly on our notes: In order to reduce their length both following this Introduction, and in the Leibniz texts themselves, we have referred to every source cited more than once by author or editor surname only; full citations are in our Bibliography.

While we have not hesitated to modify Leibnizian syntax in our translations, as noted above, we must emphasize that *all* materials enclosed within square brackets have been interpolated by us.

Finally, many of Leibniz's citations to classical Chinese texts in the *Discourse* are taken—via Longobardi and Ste.-Marie—from the *Compendium*, very little of which has been translated into a Western language. As a consequence, all references in the footnotes to classical texts are to English translations (usually Legge, who includes the original), so that non-sinologists may consult the sources as easily as Chinese specialists. On several occasions a translation of a Chinese passage is proffered in the footnotes which differ from Leibniz's texts and from other English translations of the passages; all such occasions are marked, followed by reference(s) to other translations.

Notes

1. The standard philosophical biographies of Leibniz consulted herein were those in Couturat, Rescher, and Russell.

2. See Cook and Rosemont (2) for further discussion and sources.

3. *Ibid.*

4. *Ibid.*

5. Needham, vol. II, p. 460.

6. *Ibid.*

7. Cook and Rosemont (2), pp. 146–48.

8. See the footnotes accompanying the translations for discussions of these terms, esp. fn. 19 of the *Preface,* and fn. 84 of the *Discourse.*

9. All of these themes are discussed in careful detail by Donald Lach in his "Introduction" to the *Preface* [Lach (1)], and in Mungello (1) and (2).

10. *Nouveaux mémoires sur l'état présent de la Chine,* 2 vols., Paris, 1696.

11. *Histoire de l'édit de la Chine en faveur de la religion chrestienne,* Paris, 1698.

12. Mungello (1), p. 339. Mungello's scholarly and engaging account of this dispute—indeed his whole book—should be read by everyone interested in sixteenth and seventeenth century European conceptions of China.

13. Gerhardt II, 382–83.

14. See below, note 43.

15. *Remarks,* §1, §3, and §8.

16. See especially §39 and §39a.

17. The formal sectioning was done by Kortholt but is not misleading; Leibniz described the *Discourse* in a way parallel to the sections in a letter to Rémond of 17 January 1716. Gerhardt III, p. 665.

18. Leibniz also employs regularly two other forms of argument in the *Discourse:* (1) when confronted by a Chinese passage which appears to be clearly in conflict with Christian theology, Leibniz attempts to show that similar "errors" had been made by Greeks, or early Church Fathers, scholastics, etc., without destroying Christianity, or indeed, without diminishing the respect with which such persons were treated in the Western tradition; (2) when rebutting a specific charge of Longobardi and/or Ste.-Marie against the ancients, Leibniz will point out whenever possible that the ancient texts do not explicitly state the heresy charged by the missionaries. Whatever the persuasiveness of these particular arguments from negative evidence may have been in his day, they cannot be given credence today, because most of the "heresies" deal with metaphysical and/or theological issues which were not discussed in the ancient Chinese texts at all. There being no statements about prime matter in the classical texts, for example, it follows logically, but worthlessly, that there cannot be any statements in the classical texts which contradict Christian statements about prime matter. But see also *Remarks,* §5–§8, for Leibniz's "reply."

19. E.g., in §49 and §50.

20. Bouvet's letter of 4 November 1701 suggests this view for Leibniz's binary system, and in his letter of 8 November 1702, he says that the same system, as embodied in the trigrams of the *Yi Jing,* was the basis (now lost) of music, physics, and so forth, as well as arithmetic, for the ancient Chinese. See also Mungello (2), chapter 3.

21. In §49 Leibniz says that "Confucius himself could have been ignorant about that which he did not want to investigate more deeply."

22. Gerhardt III, 549. Cited in Lach (2), p. 447.

23. Cited from Wiener (1), p. 598; original found in *Oeuvres de Leibniz* VII, 509.

24. For the general history of the European awakening to China, see the several volumes in Lach (4). On "Proto-Sinology," see Mungello (1).

25. Cited from Lach (2), p. 436; original in *Sämtliche Schriften* IV, i, 552.

26. *Sämtliche Schriften*, IV, i, 279. The *Consilium Aegyptiacum* refers to a group of documents that remained incomplete and in draft form. They were intended for, but never delivered to, Louis XIV and his advisors. The various documents were meant to enlist Louis's support for a French expedition to Egypt to relieve pressure upon the Dutch and other Protestant countries. War broke out between the English and the French in March 1672, and so events quickly superseded Leibniz's suggestions.

27. A polymath, Hermetist, and grand generalizer, Kircher believed China's civilization was derivative from Egypt's. Kircher wrote *China monumentis qua sacris qua profanis illustrata* (1667), *Obeliseus Pamphilius* (1650), and *Oedipus Aegyptiacus* (1652).

28. A summary of Müller's work is in Lach (3). For his *Clavis Sinica,* see Mungello (1) p. 198ff.

29. On Gohl, see Duyvendak.

30. *An Historical Essay Endeavoring a Probability That the Language of the Empire of China is Like Primitive Language* (London, 1669).

31. See Mungello (1) for Mentzel's work on the Chinese language. By 1679 Leibniz already seems to appreciate that the Chinese script could not serve as the basis for his "universal characteristic." In a letter to Duke John Frederick of that year he wrote:

> If you know Chinese characters, I believe that you will find a little more harmony in them, but basically they are indubitably far removed from that analysis of thought which comprises the essence of my plan, as they are apparently content to give several connotations, as do Egyptian hieroglyphics, all of which are *entre les choses.*

Cited from Lach (2), p. 437; original in *Sämtliche Schriften* I, ii, 167. But Leibniz continued to think highly of the language, as he indicated in a letter written a quarter of a century later to Bouvet (18 May 1703):

> I cannot say of the Egyptian hieroglyphics . . . that they have any agreement with the Chinese characters . . . [which] are perhaps more philosophical and appeared to be built on more intellectual considerations such as are given by numbers, order, and relations.

Cited from Wiener (2), p. 200; original found in Widmaier (2), p. 188. For further discussion of Leibniz's views of the Chinese language, especially as they bore on his philosophy, see especially Widmaier (1).

32. The history, details, analysis and evaluation of this text are ably done in Mungello (1), chapter VIII. For a biography of Father Couplet, see Heyndrickx.

33. Leibniz, *Sämtliche Schriften* I, v, 26.

34. Grimaldi's dealings with Leibniz are discussed in Mungello (2), esp. pp. 32ff.

35. In the Grimaldi–Leibniz file, *Leibniz Briefwechsel* 330, fol. 3–5 (19 July 1689); reprinted in Widmaier (2), pp. 4–7.

36. Leibniz uses this expression in a letter of 3 January 1708, in V.I. Guerrier, *Leibniz in seinem Beziehungen zu Russland und Peter der Grosse* (St. Petersburg, 1873), appendix, p. 76. Cited in Zangger, p. 190.

37. For a clearer view of Chinese astronomy, consult Sivin (1).

38. The standard biography of Ricci is Cronin. An excellent portrait of this outstanding man is in Spence (2). See also Trigault.

39. See Trigault.

40. As in our first publication of the *Discourse,* we follow Mungello (1) in referring to the Longobardi text in this way. On Navarette's translation of Longobardi's text, see Gernet, esp. p. 9ff, and Cummins.

41. About Antoine de Sainte-Marie nothing is known. His name cannot be found in other materials pertaining to Leibniz (except as the author of the *Mission Treatise*), nor in French biographical dictionaries, nor in Catholic dictionaries and encyclopedias. There are several references, however, in these works to a Spanish Franciscan named Antonio Caballero, who is also called therein Antonio Caballero a Santa Maria. The dates and activities given and described for Caballero correspond precisely with those that must be assumed for Ste.-Marie on the basis of statements and dates found in the *Mission Treatise.* Moreover, the epitaph in Canton included in Caballero's most detailed bibliography reads:

A. R. P. F. ANTONIO A S. MARIA
ORDINIS MINORUM, MINISTRO ET PRAEFECTO VERE APOSTOLICO
AB EXILIO CANTONENSI AD COEL ESTEM PATRIAM EVOCATO
ANNO M. D. C. XIX

which suggests strongly that Caballero and Ste.-Marie were one and the same. The biographies of Caballero do not, however, specifically mention his writing the *Mission Treatise,* so there remains some room for doubt. See *Sinica Franciscana,* vol. II, p. 329, and the *New Catholic Encyclopaedia* under "Caballero."

42. Again following Mungello. See fn. 40.

43. We say "apparently" here because in his letters to Leibniz of 1 April (Gerhardt III, 640) and 4 September 1715 (*Ibid.,* 641) Rémond mentions the Longobardi work, but not Sainte-Marie's, mentioning instead Malebranche's *A*

Dialogue Between a Christian Philosopher and a Chinese Philosopher: On the Nature and Existence of God (Paris, 1708). Receipt of this latter work is acknowledged by Leibniz, even though he does not cite it in the *Discourse*. He must have received the Sainte-Marie text from Rémond as well, however, because he acknowledged it in a letter to Rémond dated 4 November 1715 (Gerhardt III, 66). See the recent English translation of Malebranche's text done by Iorio. For more on Malebranche in this regard, see Mungello (3).

44. Martini was an exceptional man; he and his writings have finally received the scholarly attention they deserve in Mungello (1), chapter IV, from which much of the material on Martini herein was taken. There is also a brief biography of him in the *New Catholic Encyclopedia*.

45. A copy of which is in Leibniz's library.

46. For an interesting analysis of Ussher's work, see Gould, pp. 183–191.

47. The Leibniz–Bouvet correspondence has recently been published (but not translated) in Widmaier (2).

48. See Heeren. The portrait of Kang Xi is plate 2.

49. Leibniz's last six letters to Bouvet went unanswered, which must have disappointed the philosopher. See also H. Wilhelm (1), Mungello (2), chapter 3, and Swiderski.

50. On Figurism and Bouvet, see Secret, pp. 35–53.

51. Bouvet to Leibniz 4 November 1701; Widmaier (2), pp. 147–163.

52. *Remarks*, §9.

53. The most complete account of the "Ancient Theology" is in Walker. Chapter 6 is specifically devoted to its influence on the seventeenth century French Jesuit missionaries to China.

54. As he repeatedly does in the *Discourse*.

55. Leibniz to Herzog Rudolph August 2 January 1697, in Loosen and Vonessen, pp 19–23; translated in Ching and Oxtoby (2), pp. 70–76.

56. Translated in Walker, p. 223. The original may be found in Widmaier (2), p. 187. See also *Remarks*, §9.

57. *Preface*, §21.

58. For those who wish to learn more about the missionary work of these men and their contemporaries, see Mungello (1), and Dunne, and Rowbothham.

59. This temporal trichotomy is by no means the invention of Leibniz nor the Christian missionaries; most Chinese literati from at least the thirteenth century CE onward would outline the intellectual history of their civilization in roughly the same way, with due allowance made *a*) for the legendary nature of pre-Zhou figures, and *b*) the introduction and spread of Buddhism, which began in the first century CE.

60. While the Shang had a fairly sophisticated writing system, all extant materials are in the form of divinatory formulae or memorials, inscribed on tortoise plastrons, cattle scapulae, or the molds used to cast bronze presentation ritual vessels. See Keightley.

61. The best translation is by R. Wilhelm. See also H. Wilhelm (2).

62. Some scholars have indicated the hexagrams came first. But see Cammann.

63. Hexagrams 11 and 12 respectively.

64. Bouvet to Leibniz 4 November 1701. The original is in Widmaier (2), pp. 147–163, as well as her incisive notes and commentary which follow; see also Swiderski.

65. See *Remarks,* §9, and *Discourse,* §§71 ff.

66. Bouvet to Leibniz, 4 November 1701.

67. Although there is agreement in the Chinese historical tradition to accord Fuxi the credit for the trigrams, the tradition usually accords the honor for the invention of writing to the Yellow Emperor's minister Cang Jie (倉 頡) ca. the twenty-seventh century BCE.

68. Translated by Legge (1), vol. III, and Karlgren (2).

69. Legge (1), vol. IV. A literal translation is Karlgren's (3), and a poetic version is Waley's (2).

70. *Lun Yu* 7:11. All references to the *Lun Yu* here and in the textual notes are by Book and chapter number. For other translations see Legge (1), vol. I, and Waley (3), both of which use the same numbering system employed herein.

71. The only full biography of Confucius in English is Creel (3), now almost 45 years old, but it holds up well under the test of time.

72. *Lun Yu* 11:7, 7:22 and 9:5, 7:5, and 9:8 respectively.

73. Legge (1), vol. II.

74. Legge (2).

75. Combining these four works, and claiming them as the essence of early Confucianism, was done by Zhu Xi, who is taken up below in the text.

76. *Lun Yu* 11:11.

77. The most original philosophical interpretation of Confucius in recent years is Fingarette. See also the review article by Rosemont (1), and also Rosemont (2). Other authors who have interpreted the Analects against the background of Fingarette's work are Graham (1), Hall and Ames, Schwartz (2), and Tu.

78. Zhang Cai (張 載); Cheng Yi (程 頤), 1033–1108; and Cheng Hao (程 顥), 1032–1085. See Graham (2) for their philosophical biographies.

79. 朱熹 See Chan (2). Plate 8 is a self-portrait of him.

80. For more on these topics, see, for example, de Bary (2), Bloom, Dimberg, Tillman, and the bibliographies in these works.

81. Mungello (1). For more on the *Compendium,* see Lundbaek.

82. See note 43.

83. *Religion Treatise* 1:9. In his marginal notes to Longobardi's text, Leibniz makes reference to Sainte-Marie's bibliographic discussion, which placed the compilation of the *Compendium* as occurring 300 rather than 2,500 years earlier. It is difficult to know why and how chronological errors of this magnitude were made so frequently by the early missionary scholar/translators, especially as the Chinese tradition of scholarship consistently printed the basic texts in large type, with commentaries doubled in each line, in much smaller type.

84. Wright, pp. 100–101.

85. For more on this and related tensions in Neo-Confucianism, see Metzger. See also de Bary (1).

86. The virtues—or lack thereof—of the examination system had been debated by the literati as far back as the Tang Dynasty (618–906); it was not original with the Ming, only more intensified. An excellent treatment of these tensions is in Nivison. See also notes 77, 80, and 85 above.

87. Koln: *Deutsche China-Gesellschaft,* 1979. See also the review of the work in Cook (2). The variants are as follows:

Paragraph:
§1:   for "anuitente," read "annitente"
§1:   for "astimulante," read "astipulante"
§4:   for "si quod ratio," read "qua natio"
§5:   for "Imperatorem Lunae," read "Lunae Imperatorem"
§13:   for "ut Urania sancta," read "Uranie, ut Sancta"
§17:   for "Pequimum," read "Pekimum"
§17:   for "gentis," read "gerentis"
§20:   for "auctoritati," read "autoritati"
§21:   for "caepêre," read "coepere"

88. *Monumenta Serica* XV, 1956, pp. 328–343.

89. G. W. Leibniz, *Discours sur la théologie naturelle des Chinois* plus quelques écrits sur la question religieuse de la Chine. Paris: L' Herne, 1987, pp. 57–72.

90. Honolulu: University Press of Hawaii 1957.

91. Frankfurt am Main: Vittorio Klostermann, 1990.

92. *Studia Leibnitiana,* XVI (1984). The new (1992) English translation of *De cultu* in Ching and Oxtoby (1) appeared after we had completed our own translation. We did not use their work; we cite it for comparative purposes only, hoping that readers will also compare their translation and commentary on the

Discourse (in the same volume) with our own first edition, published 15 years earlier. We found the many similarities highly remarkable, and therefore the paucity of collegial acknowledgment thereof, regrettable.

93. von Collani, (1) p. 82.

94. See Frémont, p. 53. Frémont also has a French translation of *De cultu*; see pp. 163–169.

95. VI, 1, p. 187.

96. II, 380–384.

97. See Frémont, pp. 182–190.

98. Those reviews which assisted us the most are David Mungello's in *Studia Leibnitiana,* IX (1977); Robert Mulvaney's in *Philosophy East and West,* XXX (1980); Diogenes Allen's in *The Princeton Seminary Bulletin* New Series, II (1978); Zwi Werblowsky's in *Numen,* XXVII (1980); and Edward Machle's in the *Journal of the History of Philosophy,* XVIII, (1980).

99. Cook and Rosemont (1), pp. 39–42.

100. Gerhardt II, 508.

101. Gerhardt III, 667.

102. *Ibid.,* 675.

103. II, 413–494.

104. Kortholt calls this section of the volume "Anciens Traitez de divers auteurs sur la ceremonies de la Chine avec des notes de Leibniz."

105. *Gottfried Wilhelm Leibniz: Zwei Briefe über das binäre Zahlensstem und die chinesische Philosophie.* Trans. R. Loosen and F. Vonessen (Stuttgart: Belser-Presse, 1968), pp. 39–132. It first appeared in *Antaios* VII, no. 2, pp. 144–203.

106. What follows is a list of all the variant readings where the autograph differs from the best printed text, i.e., the Loosen–Vonessen edition. Paragraph numbers follow that edition. We have not noted the many instances where Loosen–Vonessen have either added or corrected the page numbers Leibniz noted in referring to the texts of Longobardi and Sainte-Marie. Paragraph:

§1:   for "considerable de son temps," read "considerable en son temps"
§2:   for "Philosophes et les Peres," read "Philosophes et Peres"
§2:   for "ressemblent à ces Chrestiens," read "ressemblent à des Chrestiens"
§2:   for "ou Anges ne nient," read "ou Anges avec des anciens peres ou philosophes ne nient"
§3:   for "on ne pourra pas luy," read "on ne pourra luy"
§3:   for "n'etant point encore fait," read "n'etant point fait encore"
§11:   for "se contredisent. Mais," read "se contredisent veritables. Mais"
§11:   for "refutant et rebutant," read "refutant et faison [?] rebutant"
§11:   for "la plus uniforme," read "la plus raisonnable"
§13:   for "legerement toutes leurs Ecoles," read "legerement toute leur Ecole"

§16:   for "(ouvrage des plus ordinaires chez," read (ouvrage des plus originaires chez"

§16:   for "une traduction bien," read "une transaction bien"

§17:   for "et qui entendoit parfaitement," read "et qui savoit parfaitement"

§18:   for "en les expliquant de," read "en l'expliquant de"

§20:   for "qu'il n'y en a point de," read "qu'il n'y a point de"

§21:   for "directrice et productice," read "directrice et productrice"

§30:   for "souiller les vertus et les perfections," read "souiller les perfections"

§32:   for "autant de systemes du Monde," read "autant de systemes Mondains"

§34:   for "Hiaxi," read "Hia Xi."

§34a: for "qu'il avoit eue avec," read "qu'il avoit a eue avec"

§35:   for "il confondoit des choses differents," read "il confondoit des different choses"

§38:   for "par ordre du Roy," read "par ordre Royal,"

§38:   for "il y a plus de 300 ans," read "il y a quelques plus de 300 ans"

§39:   for "separeroient l'incertain du certain," read "separeroient le certain"

§41:   for "cela étant, ainsi que seroit-ce," read "cela étant, que ce seroit ce que"

§43:   for "des esprits) ne s'ensuive. Et," read "des esprits) s'ensuive. Et"

§48:   for "des Machines preparées pour cela," read "des Machines preparées a cela"

§48a: for "parce qu'il jugeoit," read "parce qu'ils jugeoit"

§50:   for "en conclure encore, que," read "en conclure encore de ce silence affecté de Confucius, que"

§53:   for "activité ou son influence," read "activité ou influence"

§54a: for "ou si vous voulés au Li," read "si voulés au Li"

§54b: for "peuple a le droit de sacrificer," read "peuple a droit de sacrificer"

§55:   for "comme son palais," read "comme à son palais"

§55:   for "terre, sur les montagnes," read "terre, les montagnes"

§55:   for "favorable par des Sacrifices," read "favorable par ses Sacrifices"

§55:   for "que les sages se contentent," read "que sages se contentent"

§63:   for "de Dieu, de meme que les Anges," read "de Dieu, tout comme les Anges"

§64:   for "que selon les Chinois," read "que tout selon les Chinois"

§74:   for "qu'on talonne comme," read "qu'on tatonne comme." [See Zacher, p. 210, n. 378.]

Loosen and Vonessen regularly, but not uniformly, include in brackets brief passages which Leibniz crossed out in the manuscript. On only three occasions did we believe the deleted material added to an understanding of the text. See textual footnotes 14, 177, and 178.

107. See textual footnote 189.

Preface to the
NOVISSIMA SINICA
(1697 / 1699)

THE LATEST NEWS FROM CHINA

Illuminating the History of our Times, wherein is exhibited the documents sent to Europe concerning the now first officially sanctioned propagation of Christianity. Furthermore, many hitherto unknown matters are explained on the support for European Sciences, on the mores of the people and especially on the monarch himself as well as on the war of the Chinese with the Muscovites and their concluded peace.

G. G. L. greets his most kind readers:

§1　I consider it a singular plan of the fates that human cultivation and refinement should today be concentrated, as it were, in the two extremes of our continent, in Europe and in Tschina[1] (as they call it), which adorns the Orient as Europe does the opposite edge of the earth. Perhaps Supreme Providence has ordained such an arrangement, so that as the most cultivated and distant peoples stretch out their arms to each other, those in between may gradually be brought to a better way of life. I do not think it an accident that the Muscovites[2] whose vast realm connects Europe

---

[1] The early Portuguese spelling for China. The orthography, and the name, were important, for there were disputes in Europe about whether Cathay and China were one and the same. Leibniz takes up this issue again in §21. "Cambulac," spelled a variety of ways, refers to Beijing. See also §21, below.

[2] Russians. The references following are to Tsar Peter I and the Patriarch Adrian, who actually opposed Westernization, *contra* Leibniz. See Lach (1).

with China and who hold sway over the deep barbarian lands of the North by the shore of the frozen ocean, should be led to the emulation of our ways through the strenuous efforts of their present ruler and their Patriarch, as I understand it, in agreement with him.

§2   Now the Chinese Empire, which challenges Europe in cultivated area and certainly surpasses her in population, vies with us in many other ways in almost equal combat, so that now they win, now we. But what should I put down first by way of comparison? To go over everything, even though useful, would be lengthy and is not our proper task in this place. In the useful arts and in practical experience with natural objects we are, all things considered, about equal to them, and each people has knowledge which it could with profit communicate to the other. In profundity of knowledge and in the theoretical disciplines we are their superiors. For besides logic and metaphysics, and the knowledge of things incorporeal, which we justly claim as peculiarly our province, we excel by far in the understanding of concepts which are abstracted by the mind from the material, i.e., in things mathematical, as is in truth demonstrated when Chinese astronomy comes into competition with our own.[3] The Chinese are thus seen to be ignorant of that great light of the mind, the art of demonstration, and they have remained content with a sort of empirical geometry, which our artisans universally possess. They also yield to us in military science, not so much out of ignorance as by deliberation. For they despise everything which creates or nourishes ferocity in men, and almost in emulation of the higher teachings of Christ (and not, as some wrongly suggest, because of anxiety), they are averse to war. They would be wise indeed if they were alone in the world. But as things are, it comes back to this, that even the good must cultivate the arts of war, so that the evil may not gain power over everything. In these matters, then, we are superior.

§3   But who would have believed that there is on earth a people who, though we are in our view so very advanced in every branch of behavior, still surpass us in comprehending the precepts of civil life? Yet now we find this to be so among the Chinese, as we learn to know them better. And so if we are their equals in the industrial arts, and ahead of them in contemplative sciences, certainly they surpass us (though it is almost shameful to confess this) in practical philosophy, that is, in the precepts of ethics and

---

[3] For the Jesuits as court astronomers in Beijing, see d'Elia, and Sivin (1). On Chinese astronomy itself, Sivin (2).

politics adapted to the present life and use of mortals. Indeed, it is difficult to describe how beautifully all the laws of the Chinese, in contrast to those of other peoples, are directed to the achievement of public tranquility and the establishment of social order, so that men shall be disrupted in their relations as little as possible. Certainly by their own doing men suffer the greatest evils and in turn inflict them upon each other. It is truly said that "man is a wolf to man." Our folly is indeed great, but quite universal. We, exposed as we are to natural injuries, heap woes on ourselves, as though they were lacking from elsewhere.

§4   What harm, then, if some nation has found a remedy [for these evils]?[4] Certainly the Chinese above all others have attained a higher standard. In a vast multitude of men they have virtually accomplished more than the founders of religious orders among us have achieved within their own narrow ranks. So great is obedience toward superiors and reverence toward elders, so religious, almost, is the relation of children toward parents, that for children to contrive anything violent against their parents, even by word, is almost unheard of, and the perpetrator seems to atone for his actions even as we make a parricide pay for his deed. Moreover, there is among equals, or those having little obligation to one another, a marvelous respect, and an established order of duties. To us, not enough accustomed to act by reason and rule, these smack of servitude; yet among them, where these duties are made natural by use, they are observed gladly. As our people have noticed in amazement, the Chinese peasants and servants, when they bid farewell to friends, or when they first enjoy the sight of each other after a long separation, behave to each other so lovingly and respectfully that they challenge all the politeness of European magnates. What then would you expect from the mandarins,[5] or from Colai?[6] Thus it happens that scarcely anyone offends another by the smallest word in common conversation. And they rarely show evidences of hatred, wrath, or excitement. With us respect and careful conversation last for hardly more than the first days of a new acquaintance—scarcely even that. Soon familiarity moves in and circumspection is gladly put away for a sort of

---

[4] This sentence differs from the Lach translation: *ratio* should be *natio*. See fn. 87 in the Introduction for the other Latin variants from Lach's transcription.

[5] The general term for Chinese officials, and the scholar-official class even more generally.

[6] *Ko Lao* 閣老 , a Ming–Qing Dynasty term for the Grand Secretaries of the central (Metropolitan) government administration.

freedom which is quickly followed by contempt, backbiting, anger, and afterwards enmity. It is just the contrary with the Chinese. Neighbors and even members of a family are so held back by a hedge of custom that they are able to maintain a kind of perpetual courtesy.

§5   To be sure, they are not lacking in avarice, lust or ambition. In these regards what Harlequin, Emperor in the Moon in the theater, is accustomed to repeat of the Lunar people is also true of them: everything is done just as it is here (c'est tout comme icy).[7] Hence the Chinese do not attain to full and complete virtue. This is not to be expected except by Heaven's grace and Christian teaching. Yet they temper the bitter fruits of vice, and though they cannot tear out the roots of sin in human nature, they are apparently able to control many of the burgeoning growths of evil.

§6   Who indeed does not marvel at the monarch of such an empire? His grandeur almost exceeds human stature, and he is held by some to be a mortal god. His very nod is obeyed. Yet he is educated according to custom in virtue and wisdom and rules his subjects with an extraordinary respect for the laws and with a reverence for the advice of wise men. Endowed with such eminence he seems fit indeed to judge. Nor is it easy to find anything worthier of note than the fact that this greatest of kings, who possesses such complete authority in his own day, anxiously fears posterity and is in greater dread of the judgment of history,[8] than other kings are of representatives of estates and parliaments. Therefore he carefully seeks to avoid actions which might cast a reflection upon his reputation when recorded by the chroniclers of his reign and placed in files and secret archives.

§7   Until the reign of the present emperor Cam Hi,[9] a prince of almost unparalleled merit, the magistracy opposed any disposition on the part of the ruler to grant the Europeans freedom to practice the Christian religion legally and publicly until its integrity is ascertained and it is determined that there is no other way to bring to fruition the prince's great

---

[7] Reference is to a late seventeenth century comedy *L'empereur dans la lune*. See Lach (1).

[8] One of the first tasks of a new dynasty in China was the writing of a full history of its predecessors.

[9] The Qing Emperor Kang Xi. 康 熙 After the consolidation of Manchu rule following the overthrow of the Ming Dynasty in 1644, Kang Xi brought strength and stability to that rule, seen in the length of his reign: 61 years. For more on this unusual monarch see Spence (1), and fn. 20 in the *Remarks*. See also Plate 2.

and salutary decision to introduce European arts and sciences into China. In this matter he seems to me to have had individually much more foresight than all his officials, and I take the reason for his superior judgment to be that he combines European [culture] with Chinese. For he was taught from childhood in all things Chinese a discipline almost beyond the capacity of a private individual. For example, in the mandarins' examinations on the basis of which distinctions and magistracies are granted, he is considered a very acute judge. With his astonishing ability to write the characters (which to them is the highest erudition), he could even improve the composition of a petition drawn up by the most learned of Christians. So, while understanding the learning of his own people to begin with, and moreover, not being a bad judge when he first received a taste of European knowledge from Father Ferdinand Verbiest of Bruges in Belgium, of the Society of Jesus, a pupil of Johann Adam Schall[10] of Cologne—which perhaps no one in his empire had previously received—his foresight and his grasp of affairs can only elevate him above all other Chinese and Tartars,[11] exactly as if on a pyramid of Egypt a European steeple should be placed.

§8   I remember the Reverend Father Claude Philip Grimaldi, an eminent man of the same Society, telling me in Rome how much he admired the virtue and wisdom of this prince. Indeed (passing by, if I may, the comment on his love of justice, his charity to the populace, his moderate manner of living, and his other merits), Grimaldi asserted that the monarch's marvelous desire for knowledge almost amounted to a faith. For that ruler, whom eminent princes and the greatest men of the empire venerate from afar and revere when near, used to work with Verbiest in an inner suite for three or four hours daily with mathematical instruments and books as a pupil with his teacher. He profited so greatly that he learned the Euclidian theorems, and having understood trigonometrical calculations, could demonstrate by numbers the phenomena of the stars. And

---

[10] Johann Adam Schall von Bell (1592–1666). After Ricci, he was one of the most effective of Christian missionaries to China. An outstanding mathematician and astronomer, Schall was appointed to the Bureau of the Calendar in Beijing in 1630. He survived the chaos and collapse of the Ming rulers, and became a close friend of the young Qing Emperor Shun Zhi 順治 , who preceded Kang Xi. In 1658 Shun Zhi appointed Schall Imperial Chamberlain, but court intrigues caused him to lose his influence under Kang Xi's reign. See Treadgold, esp. chapter 1.

[11] The term for the Manchu people in Leibniz's time.

indeed, as the Reverend Father Louis Le Comte,[12] recently returned from
there, informs us in a published account of China, the emperor prepared a
book on geometry, that he might furnish his sons with the elements of so
great a science and the knowledge of so many truths, and bequeath the
wisdom which he had brought into his empire as an inheritance to his
realm, having in view the happiness of his people even in posterity. For my
part I do not see how more admirable resolutions could motivate any man.

§9   Now geometry ought not to be regarded as the sphere of
workmen but of philosophers; for, since virtue flows from wisdom, and the
spirit of wisdom is truth, those who thoroughly investigate the demonstra-
tions of geometers have perceived the nature of eternal truth, and are able
to tell the certain from the uncertain. Other mortals waver amid guesses,
and, not knowing the truth, almost ask with Pilate what it is. But there is no
doubt that the monarch of the Chinese saw very plainly what in our part of
the world Plato formerly taught, that no one can be educated in the
mysteries of the sciences except through geometry. Nor do I think the
Chinese, though they have cultivated learning with marvelous application
for thousands of years, and with great rewards to their scholars, have failed
to attain excellence in science simply because they are lacking one of the
eyes of the Europeans, to wit, geometry. Although they may be convinced
that we are one-eyed, we have still another eye, not yet well enough
understood by them, namely, First Philosophy. Through it we are admit-
ted to an understanding even of things incorporeal. Verbiest was prepared
to teach them this, rightly judging that it would prepare an opening for the
Christian religion, but death intervened.

§10   And now I learn by the authority of their king and through the
zeal of Hedraeus[13] and Verjus, great men in their order and nation, that
the Reverend Fathers Gerbillion[14] and Bouvet, French Jesuits, along with
four others, who are mathematicians from the Academie des Sciences,
have been sent to the Orient to teach the monarch, not only the
mathematical arts, but also the essence of our philosophy. But if this

---

[12] Leibniz mistakenly adds an *s* to LeComte's name here, which Lach reproduces, followed by
[sic!]. Leibniz repeats the misspelling in §22.

[13] Fr. François d'Aix de la Chaize (1624–1709), an initiator of the first French Jesuit mission to
China. Verjus was his secretary.

[14] Jean-François Gerbillon (1654–1707), one of the French Jesuits who travelled to China with
Bouvet. Excerpts of some of his correspondence are included in the *Novissima Sinica*.

process should be continued I fear that we may soon become inferior to the Chinese in all branches of knowledge. I do not say this because I grudge them new light; rather I rejoice. But it is desirable that they in turn teach us those things which are especially in our interest: the greatest use of practical philosophy and a more perfect manner of living, to say nothing now of their other arts. Certainly the condition of our affairs, slipping as we are into ever greater corruption, seems to be such that we need missionaries from the Chinese who might teach us the use and practice of natural religion, just as we have sent them teachers of revealed theology. And so I believe that if someone expert, not in the beauty of goddesses but in the excellence of peoples, were selected as judge, the golden apple would be awarded to the Chinese[15] unless we should win by virtue of one great but superhuman thing, namely, the divine gift of the Christian religion.

§11   There are those in Europe who have been striving with most praiseworthy love for many years to introduce this great gift of Heaven into the Chinese Empire. Such efforts have been made chiefly by the Society of Jesus, whose virtue in this enterprise deserves praise even from those who consider themselves its enemies. I know that Antoine Arnauld, long my friend and certainly among those who lend distinction to our age, has attacked them with ardent zeal.[16] He has upbraided several of their missionaries, but rather too vehemently in some ways, as I see it; for by the example of Paul they ought to be all things to all men, and the honors given to Confucius seem to have nothing of religious adoration in them. Moreover, Arnauld also attacks the Dutch and English in his *Apologie*, either imputing to all the bad faith of a few, or putting his trust in the tales of Tavernier, who was provoked by his private grievances against the Dutch, though it is well known that many thousands of men, in both Indies, have been converted to the faith by them.[17] Often one is pressed by both

---

[15] The reference here, of course, is to the cause of the Trojan War as described by Homer in the *Iliad*.

[16] Seven volumes' worth: *Morale pratique des Jésuits*, Cologne, 1669–1694. The differing philosophical views of Leibniz and Arnauld are discussed in Sleigh.

[17] Jean Baptiste Tavernier (1605–1689) was a French merchant-explorer who wrote detailed accounts of his travels. The Dutch, concerned that the Portuguese, through the Jesuits, not obtain a monopoly on trade with the "Far East"—especially Japan—did all they could to impede Tavernier's travels. As he regularly did, Leibniz is here being conciliatory toward the Dutch, *contra* the views of Tavernier and Arnauld. See Lach (1).

private advice and public authority in society to share in common praise and labor, provided that rivalry can be put aside in the interim. Reflecting on such efforts and considering the piety and wisdom of the great princes, I am not without hope that peace will be restored to Europe.

§12   Still the organization of the religious orders furnishes them an advantage of sacred missions, which the efforts of others cannot easily achieve. I could wish, however, that the matter might be managed so that a people whose conversion we intend should not know what we Christians disagree on among ourselves. For we all universally consent to those principles of the Christian faith which would insure the salvation of any people who would embrace them, so long as nothing heretical, spurious, or false were daubed on besides. Missions should be undertaken carefully after the manner of the old church: neither should all mysteries be heaped indiscriminately upon unprepared souls; nor should Christian truth be subverted in application, however pleasing this might be to a people, as Louise de Dieu[18] has complained was done in the gospels composed for the Persians. Rome, as I know, has occasionally called for abrupt halts as the result of uneasiness about unorthodox arrangements.[19] On the other hand, some persons, ignorant and unskilled in human affairs, have wished, though more learned and prudent men protested, to force on far-off Christians all the formulas of the West, an error which certainly was responsible for the ruin of the Church formerly flourishing in Abyssinia.[20]

§13   It is to be hoped that in the future the work will be done more cautiously, as Christian prudence dictates, so as to use properly the great opportunity divinely presented when the monarch of China sanctioned the Christian faith by public law, of which event the present tract gives the history. Until now the Christian observances have been tolerated rather than permitted. Nor has the favor of the Chinese and Tartar princes or the merit of our people previously produced anything better than a mere connivance in suspending the execution of the strictly kept laws against

---

[18] 1570–1642. A theologian and early Orientalist at the University of Leiden who wrote at length on this and similar subjects. See Lach (1).

[19] Most recently (1693) the injunction against the use of *Shang Di* and *Tian* as terms for "God," issued by Charles Maigrot as Vicar Apostolic in China. He was banished from China by Kang Xi in 1706. For the latter's opinion of the former, see Spence (1), pp. 79–80. On *Shang Di* and *Tian,* see the introduction, pp. 12–13. The Chinese graphs are 上帝 and 天.

[20] Following a civil war, the Europeans were banished from Abyssinia in 1632.

impious sects, among which our religion was numbered. But the emperor consulted the "will of heaven,"[21] and (as Verbiest has elegantly said in a work of his published in Chinese and in Latin) the muse Urania deigned to move the kingly mind so that our holy and truly celestial doctrine might be permitted.[22] Then the strength of our geometry, as soon as it was tasted by the king, was so much to his liking that he easily came to believe that those who had learned thus to reason might teach correctly in other things.

§14   Ricci had first shown to the Chinese at the beginning of the century what Europeans could do. Schall under the Chinese monarch and his Tartar successor publicly triumphed over the astronomy of the Chinese. While the present prince was as yet a minor, Verbiest with great acumen restored Christian affairs, previously upset by hostile passions. Then having obtained the friendship of the king when young, Verbiest discovered his resoluteness as a man. Missionaries were summoned to take advantage quickly of the good will of a prince intrigued by the pleasures of the sciences. For a while quarrels impeded the work.[23] The outcome of these was that the Portuguese, through the apostolic vicars [*Vicariis Pontificis*], won the right of naming the Chinese bishops.[24] But a further battle ensued between the bishops of Heliopolis[25] and Beirut, sent to the Orient with wide powers from the Pope, and the missionaries of the religious orders with their privileges and primacy of possession, variously supported.[26] At length the authority ["constancy" in the 1697 edition] of the Pope triumphed. When things had finally been settled, Verbiest lacked

---

[21] Leibniz uses the Latin *materialis coeli* here. The Chinese expression is *Tian ming* (天 命), which the English translation approximates.

[22] Lach (1), p. 3, discusses the reference to Verbiest here. After "Urania" Lach has "Heaven in Greek mythology" enclosed in square brackets, but the reference is to Urania as *muse* here, so we have added it, and omitted Lach's gloss.

[23] Largely between the Spanish and the Portuguese, through their emissaries in Rome, and missionaries in China.

[24] Awarded by Pope Alexander VIII in 1690. See Lach (1), and the following note.

[25] Lach adds "Baalbek" here in square brackets.

[26] The former was François Pallu (1609–1684?), appointed vicar apostolic of Fujian and administrator of all of China in 1680. The latter was Bernardino Della Chiesa (1644–1721), who accompanied Pallu to China and lost a struggle to Maigrot to succeed Pallu when the latter died in 1684. To prevent the Portuguese from altogether monopolizing the work of the Church in China, Alexander VIII also created eight new vicarates there in 1696.

nothing. And since he was esteemed above all others in the prince's mind, he persuaded the ruler that there are in fact in the doctrines of the Europeans many things to be treasured. Such an interest in foreign learning had not been shown in China since the emissary sent to the West in ancient times brought back the accursed idol Foe from the foremost island in the Indies.[27] As a result Grimaldi, of whom I have spoken, was sent to Europe to bring back men skilled in various arts. The memory of Verbiest's work remained so vivid in the Emperor's mind that in the interval between his death and Grimaldi's return his achievements were reviewed along with those of the great European doctors in the petition presented to entreat for liberty of religion.

§15   Then soon, after the five French Jesuits instructed in the mathematical sciences had penetrated from the kingdom of Siam into China, at the time against the will of the Portuguese, we were presented with a new opportunity to oblige the Emperor. The Muscovites, having with prudent moderation lured the barbarian nations one by one under their yoke into a vastly extended empire, became neighbors to the Chinese Tartars. Eventually controversies arose over boundaries. The situation was dealt with sometimes by arms, sometimes by negotiations. Finally ambassadors of both peoples met in the city of Nipchou in the realm of the Muscovites, closely attended by sizable contingents. The Chinese took with them Father Pereira, the Portuguese, and Father Gerbillon, the French Jesuit, through whose mediation a final touch was put upon the business with fortunate results: a firm peace was concluded and the ambassadors themselves avowed publicly that, in the midst of such a divergence of customs and points of view, and on the matter affecting the jealous rivalry of two hypersensitive nations, they would have been hopelessly divided had these priests not been present.[28] Thereafter, the Emperor most wisely used this success to commend the European doctors to his magistrates.

§16   A copy was made for me of the letters which Gerbillon wrote from the place of negotiations to Hedraeus and Verjus and entrusted to the

---

[27] The "accursed idol Foe" is the Buddha (Chinese *Fo* 佛). Buddhism seems to have first appeared in China about the beginning of the Christian era, but who brought it, and by what route, is not known. Thus Leibniz's reference to the Chinese "emissary to the West" is probably either to Fa Xian 法獻 (fl. ca. 380–415 CE), or Xuan Zang 玄奘 (596–664 CE), both Buddhist pilgrims to India who returned to China with numerous texts, and accounts of their travels.

[28] The Treaty of Nerchinsk (Leibniz's "Nipchou") was concluded in 1689. The negotiations are discussed in Lach (1), p. 14. Thomas Pereira (1645–1708) was attached to the court of Kang Xi.

care of the Muscovites. From these I have selected some memorable passages and placed them in the text. In addition, a brief account of the wanderings or rather journey of the latest Muscovite embassy since the peace is here attached. We expect, too, a full and fitting account from Adam Brand[29] of Lübeck, who has been dispatched home. I am adding also extracts from Verbiest's book of astronomy, printed in Chinese as well as in the Latin which I have seen; and the short letter of Reverend Father Grimaldi, chief of the mathematics faculty, dated from Goa on December 6, 1693, while en route with his colleagues to China, which already gives me hope of excellent communications to Europe; and lastly, extracts from those letters of Reverend Father Thomas,[30] the Belgian, vice-president of the mathematics faculty, informing us of the remarkable progress in Christianizing. I hope with this book to be able to rouse European courts and churches, so they may send laborers to the waiting harvest.

§17 From information received it may be gathered that Grimaldi, whom we understood to have fallen into danger on his way to Peking, is now safe again, to the great good of the common enterprise. When he left Rome, after sending ahead the greater number of the missionaries in Portuguese ships, he had determined to go by land through Muscovy. Provided with letters and a seal of the Imperial Chinese administration, which conducted military affairs at the highest level, Grimaldi also brought greetings on his journey from our great emperor[31] and the king of Poland.[32] But neither the importance of his business nor the recommendation of so many kings was enough to gain him admittance from the Muscovites. This is the same fate which the Reverend Father Aprilis,[33] whose journeys are well known, suffered shortly before.

---

[29] Secretary to Tsar Peter's Embassy to Beijing in 1693. He later published an English-language account of his travels (London, 1698).

[30] Like Schall, Verbiest, Grimaldi, and others before him, Antoine Thomas (1644–1709) worked at the imperial court in Beijing, doing work in mathematics, astronomy, and religion.

[31] The Holy Roman Emperor Leopold I (1658–1705). This sentence differs from the Lach transcription: *gentis* should be *gerentis*.

[32] John III Sobieski (1674–1696).

[33] Philippe Avril had also sought to gain from the Russians permission for a land route through Siberia to China. He published a lengthy account of his efforts and travels in Paris in 1692. See Lach (1), p. 7ff.

§18   Grimaldi had received promises from me of the *Key to Chinese (Clavis Sinica)* by Andreas Müller of Pomerania, a man most learned in Oriental matters. He traveled through Silesia seeking in vain to meet this man. Though he had few hopes of success, he believed that no stone should be left unturned in so important a matter. But peevishness contended with learning in Müller, and so I, Grimaldi, Ludolph,[34] and the Great Elector himself (now deceased, from whom Müller received the provostship from Berlin), strove in vain. Perhaps Müller esteemed his invention excessively or doubted that it should be brought to light while not sufficiently perfected, having believed that one is more credulous when ignorant. And the temperament of the man was so peculiar that he carried out the threats he had made. He is said to have burned his papers a little while before his death. By this strange action he hoped to take from us knowledge of whichever it was, his understanding or his ignorance. I judge that, as something worthy had already been accomplished, we might have hoped for more. This he could have produced if he had been helped enough. If only he had explained the whole affair frankly to those who could have understood it, he would without doubt have received the desired aid of great princes and especially of his lord. In the meantime, whatever it was (and I believe it was clearly something), he died obstinate, though otherwise good and deserving the commendation of Christian interests and missions.

§19   Now Grimaldi (I return to him), having found Muscovy closed to him, retraced his route to Genoa. From there he sailed to Marseilles and thence to Smyrna. He arrived in Persian territory, where and even beyond, my letters followed.[35] In addition to the recommendations of Grimaldi prepared for the Persian king, the Most Serene King of Poland had ordered and attached recommendations for the Reverend Fathers Vota[36] and Kochanski.[37] However, Grimaldi had already left and the letters only

---

[34] Hiob Ludolf (1624–1704) was a student of Jacob Gohl's, and, like his teacher, was an early scholar of non-European languages.

[35] One of the replies to which (dated 6 December 1693) is included in the *Novissima Sinica*.

[36] Charles Maurice Vota (1629–1715) was variously a papal emissary to Vienna, Warsaw, and Moscow.

[37] Adam Kochanski (1630–1700) was a long-time correspondent of Leibniz's. He served as mathematician to the King of Poland. See the next paragraph in the text.

reached him at Ispahan. He had hoped to go from Persia through the lands of the Usbek Tartars and Bokhara onward to China. In this he was deterred by the bandit-infested roads of that savage land, and held to the more frequented way of Goa, the Indies and the port of Macao. And to the great joy of the prince he was received with the highest honor in the Chinese Empire.

§20   Now Christian affairs are said to be greatly prospering with hopes high for further progress; especially if what Reverend Father Adam Kochanski (an able humanist, learned in affairs and especially in knowledge of mathematics, and a brilliant even in the star-studded company of the Jesuit order) wrote to me is true, namely, that the heir to the empire had acquired some knowledge of European languages. Already additional missionaries are being sent from France. I hope that Germany also will not fail in its duty both to itself and to Christ. In letters written to Vienna I have expressed the wish, through the Reverend Father Menegatti,[38] the imperial confessor whose eminent learning equals [corresponds to, in the 1697 edition] his authority, that—the Emperor, in his deep piety and wisdom, having recently concluded a treaty with the Muscovites—the door might be opened for sending heralds of the Gospel to China. If this enterprise appeals to the hearts of those who can aid it, I think advice can be given so that we can make proper use of divine aid and favorable circumstances.

§21   In earlier times the Chinese already began to hear of Christ. They were known by the name "Seres" [silk] to the Romans and Greeks. In the days of the great Justinian weavers brought silkworms into the Roman Empire. At the same time, particularly the monk Cosmas Indicopleustes was writing informatively about distant peoples.[39] From these writings Holstenius[40] has published an excerpt, the inscription of Adulis in interior Africa. This same Cosmas did what no one had done before by setting down the true name for the silk lands. For he called them Tzin, a pronunciation that is much more nearly correct than our vulgar one, when we refer to them as Sinas or China, or even Tschina as I have expressed it

---

[38] Francis Menegatti (1631–1700) was Professor of Theology at the University of Vienna and confessor to Leopold I.

[39] A reference to an early sixth century text, *Universal Christian Topography.* See Lach (1), p. 83.

[40] Lukas Holste (1596–1661) was Vatican librarian under Pope Innocent X. The reference is to a Greek inscription on a monument found in Adulis which, according to Lach (1), p. 83, was not in the interior of Africa, but on the Red Sea.

above in the Portuguese manner.[41] Moreover, we know that Christians from Syria penetrated to China and founded a Church there. The testimony for this is inscribed on a monument discovered in our century in China.[42] Athanasius Kircher has published the inscription and Andreas Müller has commented on it. When this discovery was received dubiously by scholars, Melchisedech Thévenot,[43] royal librarian of France, while working with great erudition and distinguished judgment primarily on a question of geography, found in the writings of the Mahometans support for its authenticity. This I am afraid may be forgotten with the death of the man. As a result of further investigation I learned that Herbelot,[44] the Frenchman most informed on Oriental subjects, who is now dead, translated a certain account (in Arabic or Persian) for the Grand Duke of Tuscany. It concerns a journey through the Usbek lands to Cathay or China, and is said to contain proof of the antiquity of Christianity in China. I have advised the eminent Antonio Magliabecchi, frequently mentioned in the writings of myself and others, to publish this work since it concerns Christian affairs. Whatever he may rescue from oblivion will doubtless find favor with the Grand Duke, whose piety equals his wisdom.[45]

§22   Since the death of Andreas Müller, the study of sinology is being continued here in Germany at Berlin by Christian Mentzel, royal physician to the most Serene and Potent Elector. His efforts are inspired by the favor and encouragement of the most wise Elector, who bows to no one in his ardent zeal for the propagation of true piety and belief. Furthermore, when I received the account by the rector of the College at Peking [Joseph Suarez], which was sent from Peking by the Reverend Father de Amarat[46]

---

[41] See fn. 1, above.

[42] I.e., the Nestorian stele in Xian.

[43] Thévenot (1620–1692) collected and published numerous manuscripts, but the later remark by Leibniz suggests that the statement of the "Mahometans'" (Muslims') support for the authenticity of the Xian stele was not among them, and Lach was not able to find such a reference either. Lach (1), p. 84.

[44] Barthelemy d' Herbelot de Molainville (1625–1695) was another early student of oriental languages, his major work being published only posthumously (Paris, 1697).

[45] Apparently the work was not rescued from oblivion. See Lach (1), p. 85. Antonio Magliabecchi (1633–1714) was librarian for the Grand Duke of Tuscany, Cosimo III (1670–1723).

[46] Lach (1), p. 85, hypothesizes the reference here must be to Father Michel de Amaral (1656–1730), a missionary to China who returned to Europe in 1694.

of Portugal with a recommendation to Herr von Cochenheim,[47] the adviser of the most reverent Bishop of Münster, I thought it concerned Christian affairs to possess an accurate picture of divine beneficence so opportunely granted.[48] I have therefore included this narrative to amplify the matters touched upon by the Reverend Louis Le Comte in his French narration of Chinese affairs. Nor do I think I have acted unwisely in adding a preface to materials relating to the prosecution of this greatest of enterprises, about which European piety is more and more inflamed. Certainly the size of the Chinese Empire is so great, the reputation of this wisest nation in the Orient so impressive, and its authority so influential an example to the rest, that scarcely since apostolic times has any greater work appeared for the Christian faith to accomplish.

§23 May God provide that our joys be solid and lasting, undisturbed by imprudent zeal, by internecine conflicts among the men traveling on apostolic duties, or by our own unworthy example.

---

[47] Councillor to the prince-bishop of Münster, 1694–1699. This section differs from the 1697 edition, wherein a person was mentioned by Leibniz, and objected thereto. See Lach (1), p. 85. See also *Remarks* §6 and *Discourse* §7.

[48] A reference to Kang Xi's 1692 Edict of Toleration for the foreign missions.

Plate 5. Confucius (© The Field Museum, Neg. #A-35933, Chicago)

On the Civil Cult of Confucius
(1700 / 1701)

§1 When I wrote the Preface to my *Novissima Sinica,* I was inclined to believe that when the Chinese literati render honors to Confucius, they consider it a civil ceremony rather than a religious cult. Since then, an opposing statement has come into my hands,[1] published by people, who though deemed well intentioned, have not all the same persuaded me [to change my mind].

§2 A religious cult (if one is searching for a definition) is, if I am not mistaken, one where we attribute to he whom we honor a superhuman power, capable of granting us rewards or inflicting punishments upon us. It matters little whether this power is in the being worshipped, as with the gods of the Gentiles, or rather in being able to intercede with God, as the saints for most Christians.

§3 In the cult which the Chinese display towards Confucius and other deceased worthy of merit, especially their own ancestors, it apparently happens that there are rites which many elsewhere would view as religious ones. But it is quite certain that these symbols are mostly so ambiguous that their veneration can be seen as some sort of political cult, like emperors— even Christian ones—who employ the name of the divinity. We indeed know the Chinese people have gone to more extremes in ceremonial pomp

---

[1] Le Comte's popular book defending the Jesuit position, was published in 1696—before the *Preface* was written—and Le Gobien's in 1698. The Jesuits were attacked from a number of sources, especially by members of the Société des Missions Êtrangères in Paris, and it is probably to one of their denunciations that Leibniz is referring here. On the other hand, it has been suggested that the "opposing statement" came in a letter to Leibniz from Antoine Arnauld. See Klutstein-Rojtman and Werblosky, p. 94.

than other nations, and in this regard they have fallen into excess. But such excesses do not require a strict interpretation.

§4   For example, when they call the place where the image of the deceased is displayed and to whom gifts are offered a "throne" or "seat" of the soul or spirit,[2] this can be easily understood in an anthropomorphic or poetic fashion as describing the glory attributed to immortality, and not as if they think the soul actually returns to this place and rejoices in the offerings.

§5   Therefore one must examine their opinions on souls[3] on the basis of the appropriate evidence. This is especially important if according to the writings canonized by scholars, one could demonstrate that the literati thought that the souls of Confucius and the others were conscious of what is happening after death and that they reward those who imitate and worship them and punish those who scorn them.

§6   As for the accounts of the anti-Jesuit missionaries, it seems to me that one can conclude that the Chinese view such veneration towards ancestors and people of great merit as advantageous so that those who practice the cult expect some benefit from it. However, they could with equal justice believe that every act deemed a virtue by the sages—and among them gratitude is not the lowest—confers considerable happiness on humankind,[4] either because this is itself the nature of the human condition or, more likely, because of a superior power providentially governing all. But it is not as if they attribute this power to the souls themselves.

§7   To be sure, it is not hard to believe that many Chinese inform all this pomp with superstition which is what greatly disturbed the Jesuit Longobardi and Navarrete of the Dominicans, as well as the French

---

[2] The Chinese expression Leibniz is referring to is *shen wei* (神 位 , "spirit seat." The common binome in Chinese *gui shen* (鬼 神) is usually translated as "ghosts and spirits." *Gui* (鬼) is properly "ghosts," connoting troubled, and mischievous entities, often demons. *Shen* (神) has only favorable connotations, referring to pure and intelligent spirits. Both terms have been used together as equivalent for "human soul." Leibniz discusses these terms at greater length in the *Discourse.* See especially §36 and §57, and the notes thereto.

[3] Again, *shen.* Leibniz more frequently uses "soul" (*anima*) than "spirit" (*spiritus*).

[4] Happiness, and social order as well: "The Master said it is upon observance of the rituals that the regulation of a state depends." (*Lun Yu* 11:25.)

missionaries for the secular clergy. But unless such perverse interpretations are officially approved, or a scandal feared, those who participate in these innocuous rites are not wrongfully engaged.

§8   As of now, I do not know if it is sufficiently clear what in fact is the authentic doctrine of the Chinese literati (especially of the classical ones), officially approved, based on their classical texts. In any event, one can hardly evaluate it properly in Europe until Chinese literature is no less familiar than the Rabbinical or Arab, so that it is possible for us to read their books and judge them critically, something that could indeed be done in Christendom.

§9   In the meantime, even if it is regarded equivocally, it is advisable to give it the most favorable meaning—as the Apostle Paul is said to have done in taking the altar erected to an unknown god as having been instituted by the Athenians for rites which they ought to have celebrated rather than for those which they usually practiced.[5] It would be rash to declare war ἄσπονδον[6] on the Emperor and the Chinese sages, as if they were accused of atheism. I praise the foresight of Matteo Ricci, a great man, for following the example of the Church Fathers who interpreted Plato and other philosophers in a Christian fashion. Let us suppose he didn't understand properly—may we not for this reason retain their opinions, like gold, purged of all impurities? If we ever impute to Confucius doctrines that are not his, certainly no pious deception would be more innocent, since danger to those mistaken and offense to those who teach is absent.

§10   Therefore, I do not think that what the Reverend Father Bouvet also indicated to me—that he had been enlightened to interpret the very ancient Chinese characters of the Book of the Ye King[7] according to the rule of true wisdom—should be made light of as I see has been done in the statement from Rome against the Jesuits.[8]

---

[5] Leibniz uses this example several times, and it is most likely taken from the *Confucius Sinarum Philosophus* . . . Ricci saw himself as imitating St. Paul's example. (Acts 17:22–34.) See also von Collani (1).

[6] "Without truce." Greek is in the original.

[7] The *Yi Jing*.

[8] In the margin here, Leibniz wrote, and then crossed out, "Hist. cult., p. 156", a reference to the *Historia cultus Sinensium* . . . (Coloniae, 1700); which Leibniz had in his Library.

§11   It is not absurd for discerning Europeans (such as Ricci) to see something today which is not adequately known by the Chinese erudites, and to be able to interpret their ancient books better than the erudites themselves. Who does not know in our own day that Christian scholars are much better interpreters of the most ancient books of the Hebrews than the Jews themselves? How often strangers have better insight into the histories and monuments[9] of a nation than their own citizens! This is even more likely concerning doctrines more than twenty centuries removed from the Chinese, who are quite possibly not as equipped with the interpretive aids as we, informed about Chinese literature, and especially aided by European methods.

§12   As to the question[10] whether it is permitted for a Chinese Christian to say Tien—heaven—for God (which is done frequently in Europe) or to call God, Xangti, supreme ruler—the term employed by the Chinese literati—is a matter, I think, for closer examination. Certainly, the opponents of the Jesuits take this for granted since the Chinese Emperor wrote on a tablet in his own hand King tien[11] ("revere Heaven")—the sort of inscription which the Jesuits then exhibited in their Churches. From this and from the Chinese themselves, one can think of heaven as visible or material. But what if the Jesuits elicited another interpretation from this or other literary expressions, especially about the supreme power who rules over heaven itself? It is thus unfair, in a matter not sufficiently clear, to condemn the Chinese without a hearing.

§13   In the meantime, if the Christian teachers, agreeing to certain formulations among themselves, would inculcate the neophytes and warn them of the danger of false interpretations and, professing them in public and in writing, moreover attest to the spirit with which the latter perform the accepted ceremonies of the people, and they [i.e., the Christian teachers] do carry it off, it will become evident that the Chinese themselves understand better than was thought, or at least that their public doctrines

---

[9] "Monument" here is possibly a reference to the Nestorian stele from Xian. See the *Preface,* §21.

[10] I.e., the "Terms Question." See the Introduction, p. 3. *Tian* and *Shang Di* were used by Ricci as lexically equivalent to "God," but his claim was vigorously disputed by others, especially Longobardi and Sainte-Marie. Leibniz discusses these terms again in the *Remarks,* and at length in the *Discourse.*

[11] *Jing tian* (敬 天).

demand no more than what we are able to concede. This is the reason I said at the time in the *Preface* [to the *Novissima Sinica*][12] why I so favor the advancement of this mission; and why it is not surprising I am pained by the obstacles set from the side where they are least deserved.

---

[12] Especially in §11, §13, and §22.

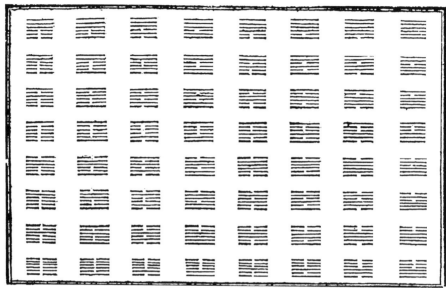

Antiquissi-
mæ Sinarum
libri

Habent. Sinæ librum Y E K I N G dictum, qui totus in his figuris explicandis est; magni apud eos pretij ob ces arcanas, quas illic latére sibi persuadent. Mihi quædam philosophia mystica videtur esse Pythagoricæque persimilis . etsi multis seculis prior; quippe quæ initium habuit a Fo Hi o, de quo dicemus infrà. Multa sunt in eo libro de generatione & corruptione, de fato, de astrologiâ iudiciariâ, de quibusdam principijs naturalibus. Sed ea jejune disputantur & exi-

Plate 6. The 64 hexagrams of the *Yi Jing* (from Martino Martini's *Sinicae Historiae decas prima* [Munich, 1658]

Remarks on Chinese Rites and Religion
(1708)

§1   Recently while looking for something in the *Journal des Savants*, which has been published in Paris for many years, my eyes fell by chance on some reviews, which I had once read, of certain books on the cult of the Chinese that had appeared long ago, that the Directors of the Seminary for Foreign Missions in Paris had taken the trouble to reissue. In the journal of 11 April 1701, the essay of Father Longobardi, S.J., who succeeded Passio, Ruiz and Sabbatinus[1] of the same missionary order, states—against Pantoja and Banoni[2]—that the Chinese have had no notion of incorporeal beings and therefore God, the Angels and the soul were unknown to them and that the substance which they call Xangti is not what we take to be God.[3] For them, all things come from a certain principle called Taikie,[4]

---

[1] François Pasio (1554–1612) had entered China with Ricci in 1582. Jean Ruiz (1561–1633) and Sabatino De Ursis (1575–1620) were colleagues of Ricci and Longobardi in Beijing.

[2] Didace de Pantoja (1571–1618) was a Spanish Jesuit who had made the trip North to Beijing with Ricci, and Alfonso Vagnoni (1568–1640) arrived shortly thereafter.

[3] Shortly after Longobardi had been appointed by Ricci as his successor to head the Mission, he began what eventuated in the Rites Controversy by calling for opinions from the other missionaries in Beijing as to whether the Chinese had a conception of God, spirits, and souls analogous to those of Christians. The first three men named by Leibniz above—Pasio, Ruiz and De Ursis—wrote treatises arguing the negative, the latter two affirmed Ricci's views. See Rowbotham, chapter X.

[4] *Tai ji* (太 極), lit. "highest ridgepole," is usually translated "Supreme Ultimate." It was a key term in Neo-Confucian metaphysics. See the two following notes.

which contains in itself the L̲i̲[5]—the primary matter as the substance of things—and the primitive ether as the proximate matter.[6] From the Li, taken in itself, emanates justice, wisdom and the other virtues; but from the Li, taken as (more) modified and thus united with the primitive ether, originates the five elements[7] and the physical forms. Ever since the beginning of the Empire, the Chinese have worshipped spirits and sacrificed to them, first, to heaven; next, to the spirit of the six causes—of heat, cold, dryness, wetness, the sun and the stars; thirdly, to the spirits of the mountains and rivers; fourthly, to the spirits of distinguished men. These spirits are composed of the same substance as the things with which they are united, have a beginning and would also end along with the world, being precisely of the same (level of) perfection—quite limited, since they are without life, knowledge or freedom. The Chinese literati are atheists: they believe the world is the result of chance; all is governed (according to them) by the random motion of bodies and the souls of the departed return into the vacuum of the first principle.

§2   On 18 April an appendix followed which contained an essay of the Dominican Father Sarpetri[8] of the Order of the Predicants against the writings of Father Longobardi on the one living, true God known to the

---

[5] *Li* (理), "Principle," "Form," "Reason" was another key term of the Neo-Confucians, at times used interchangeably with *tai ji*. Leibniz discusses *Li* at greater length in the *Discourse,* especially §4–§22. See also the footnotes to these paragraphs, esp. fn. 39.

[6] The "primitive ether" is *qi* (氣), well translated here. It has also been rendered as "air," "breath," "force," and "matter." Originally used to denote the *élan vital* in human beings (as e.g., in the *Mencius*), *qi* was developed by the Song thinkers as the complement (force/energy/matter) of *li* (form/principle/reason). At other times Leibniz translates *qi* as "primal air" and "matter" in the *Discourse*. The term is probably best glossed, and simply transliterated. Leibniz continues his discussion of these terms in §8, and extends it considerably in the *Discourse*. The origin and evolution of these and related concepts in Chinese thought is taken up in Chan.

[7] Until recently, *wu xing* (五行) was translated as "Five Elements" because the five are earth, air, fire, water, and metal. Their employment to describe the world goes back at least as far as the fourth century BCE. *Xing*, however, does not mean "elements," as that term implies matter. Rather does it mean "conduct," "motion," "ability," and "acceptable." Hence the five should best be construed metaphysically as descriptive of cyclic stages of change, hence the expression "Five phases" is now common among sinological scholars.

[8] Domingo Maria di Sarpetri (1623–1683) was one of the few Dominicans in China who sided with the Riccian accommodationists among the Jesuits.

ancient Chinese. According to Sarpetri, it is likely the ancient Chinese thought Xamgti[9] had been the name of the sole true God—and first attributed 500 years ago to the idol Chum-ti[10]—and that certain Chinese scholars so understood it, having read the book of Mattei Ricci. Ricci, a man of the greatest discernment, was ignorant of nothing which Longobardi, his successor, recounted. Since one could not invent new terms, only received Chinese words—in a purified sense—were fit to be used. Unfortunately, Longobardi had confused Zoroaster with the most ancient emperor, Fo-hi.[11] So says Sarpetri whom the other Dominicans disparaged as he was sympathetic to the Jesuits.

§3 On 25 April the essay of the Franciscan, Antoine de Ste.-Marie, was reviewed in the same journal.[12] He claims that the Chinese revered three lawgivers: Confucius, Foë and an old man who had come from the womb with completely white hair[13]; that music, perfumed fragrances, libations of wine, animals and finally expressions of thanksgiving were offered as sacrifices; that even modern teachers prostrated their bodies to the ground to honor Confucius; and that Martini,[14] in Rome in 1656, had concealed the truth. Temples and sacrifices had existed 2,000 years before Confucius, instituted by Emperor Kun, who was the fifth since the foundation of the empire.[15] At that time, the honoring of departed

---

[9] I.e., *Shang di.*

[10] It is not clear what "Chum-ti" refers to, owing in part to the nonstandard orthographies employed by Leibniz and the Chinese missionaries. The context suggests strongly, however, that Sarpetri was aware of the historical fact that the Song Dynasty Emperor Hui Zong (徽 宗) (r. 1101–1126) accorded the title *Shang di* to the Jade Emperor Yu Huang (玉 皇), one of the paramount deities of the Daoists.

[11] Longobardi was not as well steeped in Chinese thought as Ricci, but he was no novice either. It isn't clear that he confused Zoroaster and Fu Xi; in the *Religion Treatise* 2:18 he attributes to Ruiz the identification of the two.

[12] I.e., the *Mission Treatise.*

[13] The "old man . . ." here is *Lao Zi* (老 子), purported author of the book of the same name, also called the *Dao De Jing* (道 德 經). The expression *lao zi* simply means "old one" or "old philosopher"; a legendary figure.

[14] See Introduction, pp. 15–16.

[15] Although usually considered seventh or eighth rather than fifth in succession, "Kun" here probably refers to the legendary Emperor Shun (舜), r. ca 2255 BCE. In *Confucius . . .* , Father Couplet explicitly cites Shun as one who reverences *Shang di.*

ancestors was decreed, which Confucius had thereafter strongly approved. Lights, flowers, libations of wine, numerous genuflections, and prayers were offered with the purpose of gaining earthly happiness. The rite finished, the leader of the ceremonies thanked the audience in the name of the ancestors and promised prosperity to all. The same author believes that the opinion of Father Antoine of Govea,[16] that Xamgti denotes the true God, is indeed not to be ignored, but nevertheless he deems the contrary to be more likely certain. Xamgti is seen to be the dominant force in the material heavens, who reveals himself in the aereal virtues of generation and corruption. In generation, they are called emerging spirits; in corruption, returning ones. These spirits are none other than the qualities of motion and rest of the[17] Li. The Chinese appropriate a certain spirit as a patron for themselves, but this is to be likened to the Stoics for whom there is a corporeal god diffused throughout all things. Father Emanuel Diaz[18] was also opposed to the cult of the Chinese, and especially condemned sacrifices which were only for God. So read the reviews of the authors about which I will say what seems to me the likely truth.

§4   How far the civil ceremonies can be extended and by which "religion of thanksgiving," so to speak, can heroes or men of great merit be honored, I leave to the theologians for analysis. It is well established that, at one time, it was usual among Christians at the feast of St. Catharine, celebrated by philosophers, for much to be said in honor of Aristotle, even though there were no ceremonies.[19] However, we know that no people are more given to ceremonies than the Chinese, and their customs should not be judged by ours. Worship depends not so much on rites as on feelings. Therefore, one must carefully weigh in what spirit the

---

[16] Antonion de Gouveia (Gouvea, 1592–1677) was a Portuguese Jesuit long resident in China; he was a member of the group that first translated the Four Books, and his views are regularly cited by Sainte-Marie in the *Mission Treatise*.

[17] For some reason, Leibniz uses the Greek—τοῦ—as the definite article here.

[18] 1574–1659. He followed Longobardi in opposing Ricci's views. He wrote on astronomy for the Chinese court.

[19] This feast is celebrated on November 25 in veneration of St. Catharine of Alexandria, martyred in the fourth century CE, according to Christian tradition. Known for her great learning, she was the patroness of theologians, philosophers, and lawyers, and, during the medieval period, of the University of Paris.

Chinese worshipped their ancestors or those of great merit, especially whether they believed they were understood by those whom they worshipped and whether they demanded or expected something from them. From the fact that the worshippers of ancestors expect benefits promised by the priests, it does not follow that they expect them from the departed, since these benefits can originate from a higher cause who is pleased by gratitude, just as with Moses, God promises long life to those honoring father and mother.

§5   I prefer to consider what is of more concern to philosophy (i.e., natural theology), namely what is indeed to be decided about Xamgti and the spirits of the Chinese. What the ancient priests and philosophers of China thought is not easy to determine. Even with so much illumination from history, criticism and philosophy, we know how often we argue among ourselves about the meaning of Plato, Aristotle and even Augustine. Among the Chinese, I believe, neither history nor criticism nor philosophy are sufficiently developed. No one at all has yet emerged who has produced a literary history of the Chinese and who has attributed the true works, meanings and sense to each author. I also fear that the ancient texts suffer interpolations. Consequently, as a general rule, nothing prevents us from thinking well of the ancient doctrines until we are compelled to proceed in any other ways. At least their most venerable precepts of life hold out the strong hope of actually [being] doctrines of a religion of salvation. And that Longobardi denies that doctrines about incorporeal substances or rewards and punishments after this life can be elicited from the writings of Confucius must not at all disturb those who consider that no opus of the doctrines of the man exists, only that collected by his disciples, which one may term Confuciana, so far as rules of life are concerned. Indeed, neither in the books of Moses nor in the other books of the Old Testament are incorporeal substances or rewards in another life sufficiently discussed.

§6   I do not at all doubt that the Chinese literati who are atheists and who are of the opinion that all occurs by chance differ from the officially accepted religion and the spirit of those by whom it was instituted—even to the point that I doubt that they were brave enough to reveal their own [views], especially under the Emperor Cam-hio.[20] Why indeed spirits, why

---

[20] Kang Xi. Leibniz's instincts in consistently praising this monarch were justified, given Leibniz's arguments on behalf of a natural theology in China. Happily for posterity, this remarkable ruler

was there a cult of spirits—if everything happens by the bare motion of matter, if spirits cannot acquire knowledge? Although Epicurus allowed for idle gods, it is assumed that this was done more in word than in spirit. An official cult was never instituted by the Epicureans. Nor would the Chinese have worshipped ancestors or those of great merit unless they had thought this pleasing to a higher power.

§7   I would think that no doubt many philosophers from the Orient, no less than the Platonists and Stoics, regarded God as the World-soul or as the universal nature immanent in things; that other spirits also assumed bodies; and that some even considered the soul as a particle of the divine aura, which would return to the Ocean of souls with the body's death. I would not deny that this had been the thought of many Chinese philosophers, but since the philosophy of the Chinese has never been organized in a systematic form, and, I very much suspect, they lack philosophical terminology, nothing prevents interpreting what the ancients teach about divine and spiritual things in a more favorable sense.

§8   What Longobardi himself reports of the Taikie, the Li—and the primitive ether or spirit, which at least corresponds somewhat to the Trinity of the Christians or of the Platonists—supports this. The Taikie is the power or first principle; the Li is wisdom which contains the ideas or essences of things; the primitive Ether is the will or desire—what we call spirit—from which activity and creation is effected. Not for nothing are the virtues said to emanate from the Li, from which you may know that in it is the source of the true and the good. That they in fact conceive the Li or spirit as the matter of things, may have originated from the unsuitable

---

has been the subject of a study by a remarkable historian. Jonathan Spence reconstructs autobiographical remarks by Kang Xi on this issue as follows:

> On the question of the Chinese Rites that might be practiced by the Western missionaries . . . I had agreed with the formulation the Peking fathers had drawn up in 1700: that Confucius was honored by the Chinese as a master, but his name was not invoked in prayer for the purpose of gaining happiness, rank, or wealth; that worship of ancestors was an expression of love and filial remembrance, not intended to bring protection to the worshipper; and that there was no idea, when an ancestral tablet was erected, that the soul of the ancestor dwelt in that tablet. And when sacrifices were offered to Heaven it was not the blue existent sky that was addressed, but the lord and creator of all things. If the ruler Shang-ti was sometimes called Heaven, *Tien*, that had no more significance than giving honorific names to the emperor.

Spence (1), p. 79.

terminology among a people lacking in metaphysical vocabulary. Perhaps the ancient authors understood each thing to have its being and perfection from God, even though they were not able to clearly expound the means of origination.

§9 And thus, as far as I understand, I think the substance of the ancient theology[21] of the Chinese is intact and, purged of additional errors, can be harnessed to the great truths of the Christian religion. Fohi, the most ancient prince and philosopher of the Chinese, had understood the origin of things from unity and nothing, i.e., his mysterious figures reveal something of an analogy to Creation, containing the binary arithmetic (and yet hinting at greater things) that I rediscovered after so many thousands of years, where all numbers are written by only two notations, 0 and 1. So:[22]

	0	1	10	100	1000	10000	etc.
signify	0	1	2	4	8	16	etc.

The numbers are expressed as follows:

binary	decimal
0	0
1	1
10	2
11	3
100	4
101	5
110	6
111	7
1000	8
1001	9
1010	10
1011	11
1100	12
1101	13
1110	14
1111	15
10000	16
etc.	etc.

Figures of Fohi

binary	figure	binary	decimal
0	--	0	0
1	—	1	1
00	==	0	0
01	==	1	1
10	==	10	2
11	=	11	3
000	≡	0	0
001	≡	1	1
010	≡	10	2
011	≡	11	3
100	≡	100	4
101	≡	101	5
110	≡	110	6
111	≡	111	7

---

[21] The word "ancient" here is crucial to Leibniz's arguments: he believes the moderns have merely lost the true meaning(s) of what is contained in their oldest books—in the best Hermetic tradition. See Introduction, pp. 16–18.

[22] This outline of the philosopher's system of binary arithmetic is fleshed out in part IV of the *Discourse*. These tables and those in §71 of the *Discourse*, are reproduced exactly as Leibniz wrote them in the autographs.

The figures of Fohi[23] also signify two, four, eight, sixteen, thirty-two, sixty-four, as reproduced by Kircher and others—of which only two, four, and eight are herein inscribed[24]—which all the Chinese until now did not understand, but which the Reverend Father Bouvet correctly noticed corresponds to my binary arithmetic.[25]

§10   And therefore, if it is possible to get the Emperor to declare, in consultation with the nation's sages, Xamgti to be the Supreme Being— the source of wisdom, goodness and all other perfections; sacrifices to be directed especially to the author of all good; benefits to be expected not from the departed, but from himself; all other spirits to be created by him; souls to be immortal—or at least those teaching all this not to contradict the publicly approved doctrines of the Chinese, I think we will have succeeded and I think it is fruitless to look for trouble or objections to individual opinions. Suppose the understanding of the philosophers of the Chinese is or had been otherwise—nevertheless it is essential that sound doctrine be supported by public authority. I think this was the intention and Ricci, the chief founder of the mission to the Chinese—an especially wise man—has retained the better of it all, following the example of the Apostle Paul dwelling among the Athenians.[26]

---

[23] I.e., the trigrams of the *Yi Jing*.

[24] Leibniz inscribed the *yin* and *yang* line, then paired them, and then inscribed the eight trigrams.

[25] In his 4 November 1701 letter to Leibniz, Widmaier (2), pp. 147–169. Most Leibniz commentators have attributed to him the linking of his binary notation to that of the *Yi Jing*. This acknowledgement makes clear that the credit is Bouvet's.

[26] See *De cultu*, §9.

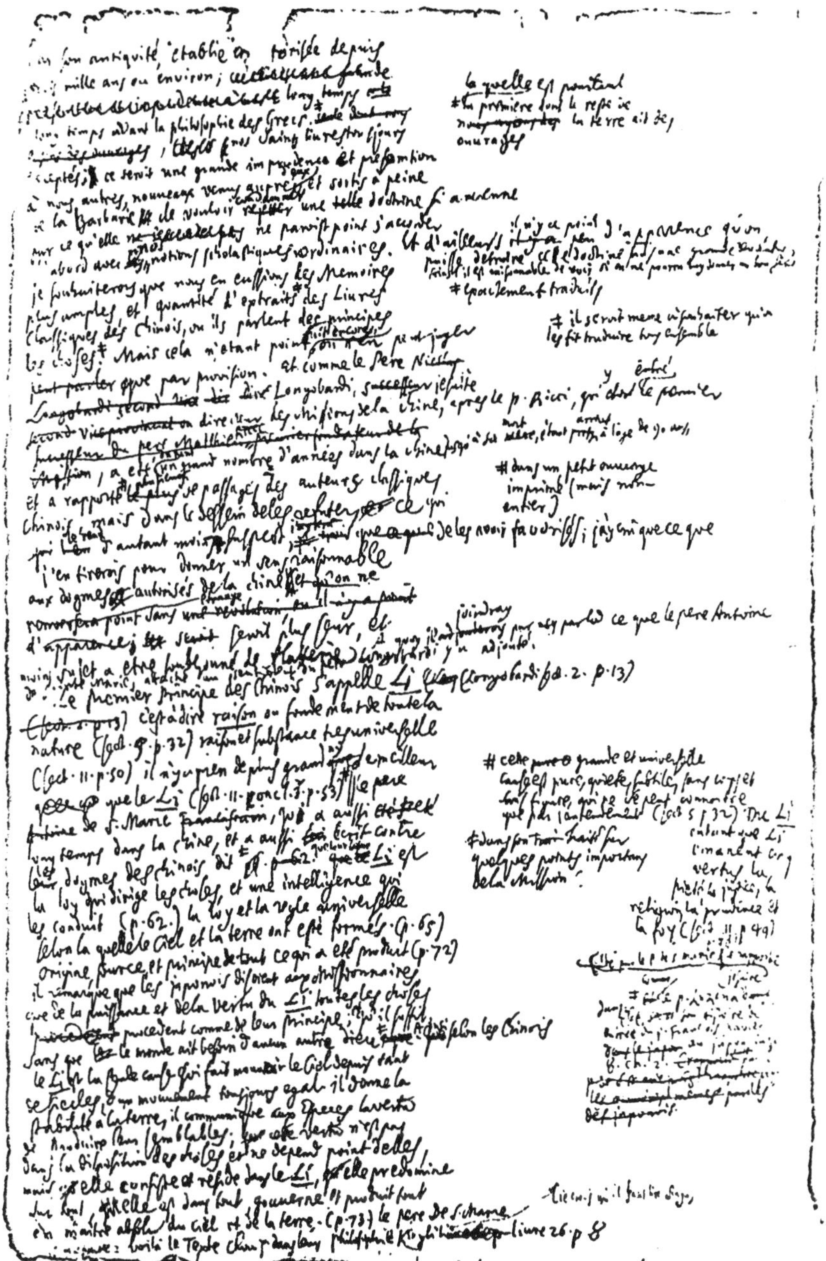

Plate 7. Page 1, *verso*, of the Leibniz autograph of the *Discourse*

Plate 8. Zhu Xi, self-portrait

Discourse on the Natural Theology of the Chinese
(1716)

[I. *Chinese Opinion Concerning God*]

§1   I have taken the pleasure of looking through the books you sent me on Chinese thought. I am inclined to believe that the [Chinese] writers, especially the ancient ones, make much sense. There should be no difficulty in granting that to them despite the opinions of some of their own modern writers. It is comparable to the Christians, who are not always obliged to follow the meaning which the Scholastics and later commentators have given to Scripture, the Church Fathers or the ancient laws. *A fortiori,* concerning the Chinese, where the Monarch, who is the leader of all sages and the living embodiment of the law, appears to reveal rational expressions of ancient doctrines. Therefore the grounds upon which Father Nicholas Longobardi (successor to Father Ricci, founder of the mission to China) most often supports himself in order to combat the accommodationist explanations of his predecessor, namely, that the Mandarins did not take such ancient writings seriously (something which made for considerable difficulty in Ricci's time), are no longer valid today by authority of this prince and many knowledgeable members of his court.[1] One should therefore profit from so great an authority. It is the proper way of correcting quite subtly, without appearing to do so, those who have strayed from the truth and even from their own antiquity. This shows that one should not be put off initially by such difficulties and that Father Martinius and those who are of his opinion, have done wisely to follow the

---

[1] Kang Xi. See *Remarks,* n.19.

advice of Father Ricci and other great men, and to maintain these explanations in spite of the opposition of Father Emanuel Diaz, S.J., Father Nicholas Longobardi, S.J., and of Father Antoine de Sainte-Marie, Franciscan, and in spite of the contempt of several Mandarins. It would be enough for the explications of the ancients simply to be sustainable because the opinions of modern Chinese appear to be ambivalent. But to examine these things more closely, these explications can, in fact, be more than sustained by the texts.[2] I speak here only of doctrine and will not examine ceremonies or worship, which require longer discussion.

§2 Initially, one may doubt if the Chinese do recognize, or have recognized, spiritual substances. But upon reflection, I believe that they did, although perhaps they did not recognize these substances as separated, and existing quite apart from matter.[3] There would be no harm in that with regard to created Spirits, because I myself am inclined to believe that Angels have bodies; which has also been the opinion of several ancient Church Fathers.[4] I am also of the opinion that the rational soul is never entirely stripped of all matter.[5] However, with regard to God, it may be

---

[2] I.e., passages from Chinese texts translated and quoted in the treatises of Longobardi and Ste.-Marie.

[3] A theme developed further in §40 and §41.

[4] The existence of the Devil and "fallen" angels is explained by several early Church Fathers as showing that certain orders of angels must possess some sort of material body, and thus, not being "essentially good," are capable both of good and evil. For example, Origen, *De Principiis*, I, v., 1–3; St. Justin (Martyr), *The Second Apology*, 5. St. Justin is quite explicit, calling the Biblical manna "angel's food" (*Dialogue with Trypho*, 57). St. Augustine speculated that God communicates corporeal actions through the medium of angelic bodies (*On the Trinity*, III, x, 21) and that the bodies of evil angels never die (*Enchiridion*, XXV, XXVI). Lactantius also believed that angels and human souls are of a heavenly fire—following Psalm 104.4. See §63.

[5] In §47 below, Leibniz states that there are an infinity of animated or ensouled substances, below as well as above human souls. The superhuman souls or spirits are called "genii," or more traditionally, "angels." No soul, whether animal, human, or superhuman is ever entirely separated from a body, even if it is a very subtle or ethereal one (§14, §20, §63), or, in a religious sense, made up of celestial fire or ether (§63, §64; see fn. 4). There are no "totally separate *souls*, nor *genii* without bodies. God alone is entirely bodiless." (*Monadology*, §72). Leibniz is always quick to note that this does not mean that a soul is nothing but an accidental collocation of material atoms (§21) or merely the epiphenomenon of some changing and perishable material substratum (§60; cf.

that the opinion of some Chinese has been to give Him a body, to consider God as the Soul of the World, and to join God to matter, as the ancient philosophers of Greece and Asia have done. But in showing that the most ancient authors of China attributed to the Li, or first principle, the production itself of the Ki,[6] or matter, one need not reprimand them, but simply explain them. It will be easier to persuade their disciplines that God is an Intelligentia supramundana, and is superior to matter. Therefore, in order to determine whether the Chinese recognize spiritual substances, one should above all consider their Li, or order, which is the prime mover and ground of all other things, and which I believe corresponds to our Divinity. Now it is impossible to understand this [correspondence] with reference to a thing purely passive, brutish and indifferent to all, and consequently without order, like matter. For example, internal order comes not from wax itself, but from whoever forms it. Also, their Spirits, which they [the Chinese] attribute to the elements, to the rivers, and to the mountains, represent either the power of God who appears through them, or perhaps (according to the opinion of some of them), they represent particular spiritual substances which are endowed with the force of action and with some knowledge, although they attribute subtle and ethereal bodies to them like the ancient philosophers and [Church] Fathers attributed to *genii* or Angels. That is why the Chinese are like those Christians who believed that certain Angels govern the elements [of earth] and the other large bodies;[7] this would be an obvious error, but would not overthrow Christianity. During the time of the Scholastics, one did not condemn those who believed, with Aristotle, that certain intelligences governed the celestial spheres. Those among the Chinese who believe that their ancestors and great heroes are among the

---

Plato's discussion in the *Phaedo*). For the reason why Leibniz held the view that "the rational soul is never entirely stripped of all matter," see fn. 130.

[6] *Qi.* See *Remarks*, n. 6.

[7] For example, Origen, whom Leibniz mentions below in another context (§60) believed that God appointed certain angels to administer the natural elements:

> For we say that the earth bears the things which are said to be under the control of nature because of the appointment of invisible husbandmen, so to speak, and other governors who control not only the produce of the earth, but also all flowing water and air. *Contra Celsum*, ed. and trans. H. Chadwick (Cambridge: Cambridge University Press, 1965), VIII, 31.

Spirits, come rather close to the words of our Lord [Matt. 22:30] which suggest that the Blessed resemble the Angels of God. Thus, it is important to consider that those who attribute bodies to the *genii* or Angels, like the ancient philosophers or early Fathers, do not thereby deny the existence of created spiritual substances, for they accord rational souls to those *genii* endowed with bodies, as also men have them, but souls more perfect because their bodies are also more perfect. Therefore, Father Longobardi—and Father Sabbatini who is cited by him—should not conclude from the fact that the Chinese appear to attribute bodies to their Spirits, that they do not at all recognize the existence of spiritual substances.

§3   China is a great Empire, no less in area than cultivated Europe, and indeed surpasses it in population and orderly government. Moreover, there is in China a public morality admirable in certain regards, conjoined to a philosophical doctrine, or rather a natural theology, venerable by its antiquity, established and authorized for about 3,000 years,[8] long before the philosophy of the Greeks whose works nevertheless are the earliest which the rest of the world possess, except of course for our Sacred Writings. It would be highly foolish and presumptuous on our part, having newly arrived compared with them, and scarcely out of barbarism, to want to condemn such an ancient doctrine simply because it does not appear to agree at first glance with our ordinary scholastic notions. Furthermore, it is highly unlikely that one could destroy this doctrine without great upheaval. Thus it is reasonable to inquire whether we could give it a proper meaning. I only wish that we had more complete accounts and greater quantity of extracts of the Chinese classics accurately translated which talk about first principles. Indeed, it would even be desirable that all the classics be translated together. But this not yet being done, one can only make provisional judgments. Father Longobardi, S.J., Director of the Mission of China—following Father Ricci (who was the first to go there)—lived in China a great many years until his death (being nearly 90 years of age). He recorded, in an incompletely published work, many passages of classical Chinese authors, but with the intent of refuting them. Since this makes those passages much less suspect of having been embroidered by him, I

---

[8] This reference to a 3,000-year-old doctrine of natural theology, coupled with Leibniz's high admiration for the trigrams of the *Yi Jing*, suggest that it is probably this classical text to which he is alluding.

believe that what I might extract from them in order to give a reasonable meaning to the authoritative dogmas of China would be more reliable, and less subject to the suspicion of flattery. In addition, I will appeal here and there to what Father Antoine de Sainte-Marie, of the same opinion as Father Longobardi, has added to them.

§4   The first principle of the Chinese is called Li (2:13), that is reason, or the foundation of all nature (5:32), the most universal reason and substance (11: 50); there is nothing greater nor better than the Li (11: 53). This great and universal cause is pure, motionless, rarified, without body or shape, and can be comprehended only through the understanding. From the Li qua Li emanate five virtues: piety, justice, religion, prudence, and faith (11: 49).[9]

§4a   Father de S.-Marie, who also lived a long time in China and has also written against Chinese doctrine, says in his *Treatise on Some Important Points of the Mission of China* that their Li is the law which directs all things and is the intelligence which guides them (p. 62). It is the Law and universal Order, according to which Heaven and Earth have been formed (p. 65); the origin, source and principle of all which has been produced (p. 72). He notes[10] that the Japanese said to the missionaries that all things proceed in their very beginning from the power and virtue of the Li. As Father Luzena,[11] S.J., cited by Father de Sainte-Marie (p. 68) records in his History of the Arrival of Father François Xavier[12] to Japan (Book 8, Ch. 2), the Li is sufficient unto itself so that the world has no need for another deity. Thus, according to the Chinese, the Li is the sole cause which always moves Heaven, throughout the centuries, in a uniform motion. It gives stability to the earth; it endows all species with the ability to reproduce their kind, this virtue not being in the nature of the things

---

[9] Longobardi gives no transliterated Chinese terms here, and is not quoting from the *Compendium*. The reference must be to the *wu chang* (五 常)—"5 constant [qualities]"—of the Confucians: *ren* (仁), "benevolence," "human-heartedness;" *yi* (義), "Righteousness," "propriety"; *li* (禮), "ritual," "rites," "worship," "etiquette"; *zhi* (智), "wisdom," "knowledge"; and *xin* (信) "sincerity," "trustworthiness."

[10] On p. 71.

[11] Fr. Joao de Lucena, S.J. (1548–1600), an early biographer of St. Francis Xavier.

[12] One of the most famous missionaries to Asia, St. Francis Xavier, S.J., (1506–1552), established missions in Goa, Japan, and Macao. He planned a mission to China, but it never materialized. He was canonized in 1622.

themselves and not depending at all upon them but consisting and residing in this Li. It has dominion over all; it is present in all things, governing and producing all as absolute master of Heaven and Earth (p. 73). Father de Sainte-Marie adds: see the Chinese texts in their Philosophy Kingli (I believe it should read Singli),[13] Book 26, p. 8.[14]

§5   In the 14th section of his work (14: 74), Father Longobardi compiles the qualities which the Chinese attribute to this first principle. They call it (par excellence) the Being, the Substance, the Entity. According to them, this substance is infinite, eternal, uncreated, incorruptible, and without beginning or end. It is not only the principle of the physical basis of Heaven and Earth and other material things, but also the principle of the moral basis of virtues, customs, and other spiritual things. It is invisible, it is perfect in its being to the highest degree, and it is itself all perfections.[15]

§6   The Chinese also call it the Supreme; or, as Longobardi says, they call it the Summary Unity because as in the number series, unity is the basis, yet is not itself a member. Also, among substances, the essences of the universe, one of them is absolutely unitary, not at all capable of divisibility as regards its being and is the principal basis of all the essences which are and which can exist in the world. But it is also the Aggregate or the most perfect multiplicity because the Being of this principle contains the essences of things as they are in their germinal state.[16] We say as much when we teach that the ideas, the primitive grounds, the prototypes of all essences, are all in God. And conjoining supreme unity with the most

---

[13] The *Compendium*. See §21, and fn. 116 below.

[14] Following this paragraph was a section struck out which reads: After all this, why not simply say that the Li is our God? That is, the ultimate, or if you wish, the primary ground of Existence and even of the possibility of things; the source of all good which is in things, the primary intelligence which was called by Anaxagoras and other ancient Greeks and Latins, Noûs, Mens.

[15] "Perfection" refers to any attribute or essential property of a thing which makes it a "perfect" example of what it is. Something is "perfect in its being" if it is wholly and completely itself, i.e., has all the properties or perfections necessary to its essential being. God is Himself all perfections (by definition) and, containing all these perfections in the highest degree, is the cause of them in other beings.

[16] Following the words "Longobardi says . . . ," up to "germinal state," Leibniz is quoting the former directly, except that all emphases are Leibniz's, and he has interpolated the emphasized phrase "the most perfect multiplicity." The expression "Summary Unity," which Longobardi refers to frequently is *tai yi* (太 一), "Great One."

perfect multiplicity, we say that God is: Unum omnia, Unum continens omnia, omnia comprehensa in uno, sed Unum formaliter, omni eminenter.[17]

§7   In the same section Father Longobardi mentions that the Chinese say that the Li is the Grand Void, the immense capacity (or Space), because this universal Essence contains all particular essences. But they also call it the sovereign plenitude because it fills all and leaves nothing empty. It is extended within and without the universe. These matters (he says) are dealt with thoroughly in the *Chung-Jung* (one of the books of Confucius) from Chapters 20 through 25.[18] In the same way we explain the immensity of God: He is everywhere and everything is in Him. So also Father Lessius has said that God is the place of things, and Mr. Guirike, inventor of the vacuum machine, believes that space pertains to God.[19] In order to give an

---

[17] "One and all, one containing all; all embraced in one; but formally one, eminently all." In late scholastic and early modern philosophy "formaliter" (formally) refers to the reality of an object apart from its being perceived or known, that is its actual existence; this compares to "eminenter" (eminently) meaning pre-eminently or in a higher degree. Thus while God is actually one, he is in a higher sense (the cause of) all. The *locus classicus* for these terms in modern philosophy is in the Latin version of Descartes's Third Meditation (*Oeuvres de Descartes,* eds. C. Adam and P. Tannery, [Paris: Cerf, 1897–1913], VII, 41), though he is distinguishing there between formal and eminent causation. "This means, for example, that a stone, which did not exist before, can in no way begin to exist now, unless it be produced by something in which there is, either formally or eminently, everything that is in the stone; . . ." R. Descartes, *Meditations on First Philosophy,* tr. D.A. Cress (Indianapolis: Hackett, 1979), p. 27, n. 4.

[18] *Zhong Yong* is about, but not written by, Confucius. The claim of authorship comes from Leibniz himself, not from Longobardi. The expression *tai xu* (太 虛)—"Great Void" or "Great Plenum"—was originally a Daoist and Buddhist term. It came into Confucian parlance with Zhang Cai (1020–1077), who used the term to denote *qi* in its uncondensed form, as pure *qi,* without form. While formless, the *tai xu* nevertheless existed, and Zhang's usage of the term was designed to combat the Buddhist view of nonexistence.

[19] Leonard Lessius (1554–1623) was a Flemish Jesuit active in doctrinal disputes within the church. Otto von Guericke of Magdeburg (1602–1686) performed an experiment in 1654 involving the creation of a vacuum by pumping the air out of hemispherical containers. Leibniz mentions this experiment (as well as Torricelli's in 1643, where he emptied the air out of a glass tube by means of mercury) in his correspondence with Clarke (Fifth Paper, §34). Leibniz, like the Aristotelians and the Cartesians, did not admit the existence of a true void and often used their arguments to support his views. *Ibid.*

appropriate sense to this, it is necessary to conceive of space not as a substance which possesses parts upon parts, but as the order of things insofar as they are considered existing together,[20] proceeding from the immensity of God inasmuch as all things depend upon him at every moment. This order of things among themselves arises from their relationship to a common principle.[21]

§8   The Chinese also call their Li a globe or circle.[22] I believe that this agrees with our way of speaking, since we speak of God as being a sphere or a circle whose center is everywhere and whose circumference is nowhere.[23]

---

[20] In his last years, Leibniz often used this same language to describe the nature of space (e.g., *Ibid.*, §29). Leibniz believed that he had sufficiently demonstrated that space cannot be real or absolute, but is purely ideal, i.e., the *perceived* mutual relations of co-existing things. Space is "only an order of things, like time, and in no sense an absolute being." (*Ibid.*, Fourth Paper, Postscript; Parkinson, p. 220.) For Leibniz's many arguments—direct and indirect—against the reality of space, see the Leibniz–Clarke Correspondence, Third Paper, §§3–5; Fourth Paper, §§7–11 and Postscript; Fifth Paper, §§27–29; 33–47.

[21] According to Leibniz, God not only created all, but sustains and governs all, through "pre-established harmony." See §14 and fn. 43.

[22] Represented by the *Yin–yang* symbol ☯ , which is also called *tai ji*, a term Leibniz uses in the *Remarks* §1. The light part of the symbol represents *yang*, the dark *yin* (see Introduction, pp. 20–21). For the Chinese these forces (principles) are complementary, not antagonistic, indicated in the symbol itself: each side penetrates the other, and each contains an element of the other within it. Longobardi discusses the relationship of *tai ji* to *yin* and *yang* at times (e.g. 5:31, 32), and Ste.-Marie does too; but Leibniz makes no mention of *yin* and *yang* in this text, and does not discuss *tai ji* in any detail. In his review of our first edition of the *Discourse* (see Introduction, n. 101), David Mungello argued plausibly that these references to globes or circles are to Zhou Dunyi's 周 敦 頤 (1017–1073) diagrams, or symbolic representations, of the *tai ji*, of which Fr. LeGobien made much in his work. See also Mungello (1), pp. 346–49, and Fung Yu-lan II, pp. 288–304. Zhou Dunyi's diagram is also reproduced in Fung, and in Needham II, p. 461. In all probability the references are to both kinds of "globe," or circle.

[23] Leibniz uses this same image for God in his *Principles of Nature and of Grace, Founded on Reason* (1714), §13. Loemker says that "Leibniz may have learned [of it] from Pascal, or from the German Rosicrucians and Theosophists." (p. 642) More specifically, Leibniz's actual source may well be Nicholas of Cusa who devotes many passages to explicating this image. In turn Cusa, or perhaps even Leibniz himself, might have learned of this image for God from the Hermetic tradition. In their edition of Cusa's works, E. Hoffman and R. Klibansky quote a passage from "Hermes

They call it the Nature of things, which I believe corresponds to our saying that God is the Natura Naturante.[24] We say that Nature is wise; that she does all for an end and nothing in vain. The Chinese also attribute to it truth and goodness as we attribute it to Being in our metaphysics. But apparently for the Chinese, just as the Li is Being par excellence so it also possesses Truth and Goodness par excellence. Father Longobardi adds that the author (I believe he means Confucius, author of the *Chung-Jung*)[25] proves his statement by referring to 18 passages from other, more ancient authors.

§8a In conclusion: Father Longobardi notes that the Chinese also attribute to the Li all manner of perfections, so that there can be nothing more perfect. It is the supreme power, the supreme good, the supreme purity. It is supremely spiritual and supremely invisible; in short, so perfect that there is nothing to add. One has said it all.

§9 Consequently can we not say that the Li of the Chinese is the sovereign substance which we revere under the name of God? But Father Longobardi objects to this (14:78 ff.). Let us see if his reasons for doing so are sufficient. I imagine (he says) that someone could believe that the Li[26] is our God because one ascribes to it those qualities and perfections which are appropriate only to God. However, do not let yourself be dazzled by these specious names under which a poisonous doctrine is hidden. For if you penetrate to the very heart of the matter, to its very root, you will see that this Li is nothing other than our prime Matter. The proof of this is that on one hand they ascribe to it grand perfections while on the other they

---

Trismegistus" written in language identical to that of Leibniz's. "Deus est sphaera infinita, cuius centrum est ubique; circumferentia nullibi." *Liber XXIV philosophorum,* prop. 2. Cited from *Nicolaue Cusanus: De Docte Ignorantia,* p. 104, notes on lines 1–3. Also see Wittkower, p. 28, n. 2. Leibniz often used notions and images of Cusa in his writings, including the notion of each creature mirroring every other as well as God, the latter "mirroring" being Cusa's explanation of God's immanence as well as an excellent example of the Microcosm–Macrocosm model that Leibniz used. See fn. 131.

[24] *Natura naturans(ante)* is the scholastic term used to distinguish the active, creative power of nature, viz., God, from *natura naturata,* created nature of substance, viz., the world.

[25] Longobardi's citation is ambiguous. See fn. 18.

[26] All underlined sentences are a direct quotation from Longobardi, except that after "Li," Longobardi has "or Tai-Kih," *(Tai ji)* which Leibniz has omitted.

ascribe to it grand imperfections as our philosophers do with respect to prime Matter. I have recorded the actual words of Father Longobardi and will examine them with care, for it appears that he is wide of the mark.

§10 I will first respond in general to the Father's comments: if the Chinese have themselves forgotten so much that they speak in a manner which appears so contradictory, one should not be assured thereby that the Li of the Chinese is prime matter rather than God.[27] Initially, one should suspend judgement and see which of the two opinions is the more plausible and whether there is not a third one as well. One should also see if they do not ascribe to the Li more of the attributes of God than the attributes of prime matter and if the first of the two doctrines does not have more in common with the rest of their doctrine. For my part, I fear that the good Father Longobardi, already prejudiced against Chinese doctrine, has himself been "dazzled" by the writings of certain Mandarin Atheists, who have ridiculed those who wish to draw consequences from the doctrines of their ancestors in order to establish the Divinity, Providence and the rest of natural religion. One should no more trust the obviously strained interpretation of such people than one would trust those of an Atheist in Europe who would try to demonstrate by passages pulled out of context, from Solomon and other holy authors, that there is no reward or punishment beyond this life.[28] And if by misfortune Atheism should prevail in Europe and become the doctrine of the most learned—as there was a time when Averroism almost prevailed among the philosophers of Italy—then if missionaries were sent to Europe by the sages of China and they studied our ancient books, they would have reason to oppose the wave of opinion of these most learned men and to ridicule their ridicule.

§11 Father de Sainte-Marie (pp. 84,85), recounting the great and good things the Chinese say of the Li, the Taikie and the Xangti, which are appropriate only to God on the one hand, but which they deprive of all

---

[27] As Leibniz says below (§12), *prime matter* is purely passive, capable only of receiving motions or shapes from an active power (e.g., forms or entelechies) and is hence incapable of the active powers ascribed to the *Li*. Without being informed with a soul or entelechy or some sort of power of activity, matter is never a genuine or complete substance according to Leibniz and can be known only in abstraction from it. Loemker, p. 119, n. 5. *Secondary matter* (see §23) refers to the matter of individual bodies subject to the various laws of physics (e.g., inertia, resistance, etc.).

[28] Ecclesiastes 9:2–5.

consciousness on the other, believes that they thereby contradict one another. But if this is the case, why do they not cling to the good which they ascribe to it, refuting and rebutting that which they say is bad and contradictory of the good? According to the Chinese, the Li or the Taikie is the One par excellance, pure goodness without admixture, a being completely simple and good, the principle which formed Heaven and Earth; it is supreme truth and strength in itself, yet not confined to itself; and in order to manifest itself, created all things. It is the source of purity, virtue and charity. The creation of all things is its proper science, and all perfections come from its essence and its nature. This principle comprehends all the ways and the laws of reason (external as well as internal to itself), by which it disposes of all in its time without ever ceasing to act or create. It can be assumed that the Li, Taikie, or Xangti is an intelligent nature which sees all, knows all and can do all. Now the Chinese could not without contradiction attribute such great things to a nature which they believed to be without any capacities, without life, without consciousness, without intelligence and without wisdom.[29] But the Father responds that pagan philosophers have also advanced things which imply contradiction. I believe that the contradictions are indeed expressed in the language they use, *in terminis terminantibus*.[30] One may, however, attribute them to different sects, not the same sect. But if they are within the same sect, one should seek a conciliation and do so in the most equitable fashion.

§12　But turning to the details [of my objection to Longobardi's argument], I do not at all see how it could be possible for the Chinese to elicit from prime matter—as our philosophers teach it in their schools, as purely passive, without order or form—the origin of activity, of order and of all forms. I do not believe them to be so stupid or absurd. This scholastic notion of prime matter has no other perfection beyond that of Being, other than that of receptivity, i.e., passive power. It has only the capacity to receive all sorts of shapes, motions and forms. However, it could never be the source of them. It is clear as day that the active power, and the perception which regulates this active power to operate in a determinate matter, are not suited to it. Therefore, I believe that it is quite inappropriate to equate the L̲i̲ of the Chinese—which is Reason or Order—with prime matter.

---

[29] See the conclusion of §16b.

[30] I.e., "in the terms to be defined."

§13   During the time of the Scholastics, there was a certain David of Dinant[31] who held that God was the prime matter of things. One could say the same of Spinoza who appeared to hold that creatures are only modes of God.[32] But prime matter in the sense of these authors is not a purely passive thing, for it contains in itself the active principle. It could be that some Chinese had similar ideas, but one cannot thus simply accuse their whole school of such ideas.[33] Among us, one often says that the soul is part of God, divinae particula aurae.[34] Such expressions require a charitable interpretation. God has no parts at all and if one claims that the soul is an emanation of God, one should not imagine thereby that the soul is a portion which is detached from Him and to which it must return as a drop of water to the ocean. Such would render God divisible, whereas in fact the soul is an immediate production of God. Some philosophers, such as Julius Scaliger,[35] have held that forms are not at all the result of matter, but the result of an efficient cause; this was sustained by the Traducians.[36] But one

---

[31] Little is known about this figure, except that he taught in Paris at the beginning of the thirteenth century. He is known as a materialistic pantheist, but our knowledge of him is mostly from other sources. He held a monistic view of reality where God, mind, and matter were essentially undifferentiated (i.e., possessed no essential forms). According to Dinant, if God and matter have no form, they are being in potentiality or prime matter. Thus, "The ultimate reality, which is at once God, mind, and matter, is best described as matter." "David of Dinant," *Encyclopedia of Philosophy*, I, 306.

[32] In Book I, Definition V of the *Ethics*, Spinoza says, "By mode I understand the modifications of substance, . . ." Furthermore, Proposition XIV of the same Book states, "Besides God no substance can be nor can be conceived." Hence *anything* which is, is a mode of God.

[33] The context here makes it difficult to tell whether Leibniz is referring to (1) all Chinese philosophers; or (2) the literati—i.e., the Confucians; or (3) those syncretistic thinkers of Ming times who were attempting to merge the "3 Schools" into one.

[34] "A particle of the divine breath."

[35] Julius Caesar Scaliger (1484–1558) was a student of the Aristotelian Renaissance scholar Pietro Pomponazzi. He is confused at times with his famous son, Joseph Justus Scaliger (1540–1609), a Greek and Roman scholar.

[36] Both Scaliger (see fn. 35) and the Traducians objected to the theory that substantial forms and souls "were derived from the potency of matter, this being called *Eduction*." (*Theodicy*, §88) Scaliger and the Traducians opposed this theory with one of *Traduction*, where souls are propagated in a similar way to the procreation of the body, thus, in effect, being transmitted by the parents to their

may not say that the soul could have emanated from the substance of God in such a way as to grant parts to God; the soul can only be produced from nothing. Consequently if some Chinese philosopher says that things are emanations of the Li, one should not immediately accuse him of making Li the material cause of things.

§14 I believe that one can take the passage from the book entitled Chu-zu (Chap. 28 of the [Hsing-li] Philosophy, p. 2) that Father Longobardi cites, in the above sense. This author [Zhu Xi] says very wisely that the Spirits are not merely air, but the force of air. And if Confucius has said to one of his disciples that the Spirits are only air, he meant animated air and was accommodating himself to the intellectual capacity of this disciple, scarcely capable of conceiving spiritual substances.[37] Thus for the Greeks and the Latins, Pneuma, Spiritus, signifies air; that is a subtle and penetrating matter in which created immaterial substances are in effect clothed.[38] The same author (book 28, p. 13) adds a little later that the Spirits are called Li. I judge that the word is ambiguous and is sometimes taken as Spirit par excellence, sometimes also as any spirit, for it may be the case that etymologically, it signifies reason or order.[39] The Chinese author, according to the translation which Father Longobardi gives us, proceeds as

---

children. Leibniz himself inclines to such a theory in a modified form to explain the origin of human souls as well as organic bodies in general.

> This production [of human souls] is a kind of *traduction,* but more manageable than that kind which is commonly taught; it does not derive the soul from a soul, but only the animate from an animate, and it avoids the repeated miracles of a new creation, which would cause a new and pure soul to enter a body that must corrupt it. (*Theodicy,* §397; Allen, 166)

[37] Here and elsewhere in the text Leibniz correctly attributes to Confucius a pedagogy that geared the Master's teachings to the intellectual and spiritual development of his students. There are many passages in the *Lun Yu* which show that Confucius did indeed evaluate the progress of his followers, but there is little evidence to suggest, as Longobardi and Ste.-Marie do, that he had an esoteric doctrine transmitted only to advanced initiates. Leibniz argues this point explicitly in §49.

[38] See fn. 4.

[39] The character 理 has two components: 王 and 里 . The former is the term for jade, and the latter is the term for the Chinese mile (about ⅓ of a mile). 里 in turn is made up of the term for field 田 , and the term for earth 土 . Chinese etymologies suggest that the compound Li of which Leibniz speaks (理) originally referred to the venation in pieces of jade, and thus came to have the meaning of order, or pattern. See Karlgren (1), §978.

follows: The Spirits are all from the same Li,[40] so that the Li is the substance and the universal Being of all things. I would imagine that he means to say that the Li is, so to speak, the quintessence, the very life, the power and principle being of things, since he has expressly distinguished the Li of the air from the matter of the air. It appears that here the Li does not signify prime spiritual substance but spiritual substance or entelechy[41] in general; that is, it signifies what is endowed with activity and perception or orderly action as souls are. And since [Zhu Xi] adds, that things have no other difference among them than that of being more or less coarse, more or less extended matter,[42] he apparently wants to say, not that the Li or Spirits are material, but that those things animated by spirits, and those conjoined to material less coarse and more extended, are more perfect. It is easy to see that this author has not penetrated enough into this issue and that he has sought the source of the diversity of Spirits in their bodies—as has been done by many of our own philosophers, who have not known of pre-established harmony[43]—but at least he has said nothing false. Thus his

---

[40] In quoting Longobardi here, Leibniz omits a phrase. In this section of the *Religion Treatise*, Longobardi is discussing the different kinds of spirits in Chinese religion, and his statement begins: "These spirits, as well as others, called *Li*. . . ."

[41] For Leibniz, every substance *qua* substance is such by virtue of an internal unifying active power or force. Leibniz uses the Aristotelian term "Entelecheia" to denote this activity (as well as a synonym for substance itself, especially immaterial ones—see §21), believing that he alone was faithful to its original sense, unlike later medieval commentators on Aristotle (see end of §38). "Entelechy" is used by Leibniz as a more inclusive term than soul, the latter usually being reserved for those substance or monads "whose perception is more distinct and is accompanied by memory." (*Monadology*, §19) Yet in other writings, such as the present text, he several times uses "entelechy" as synonymous with "soul" or "spirit" (see §21). Occasionally, if Leibniz wishes to stress the immaterial aspect of some entelechies, he adds the word "first" or "primitive" (see §19). In this sense he is conforming to Aristotle's distinctive use of "first entelechy": (*De Anima*, II, 412a, 20–29) as the *form* or *actuality* of living, natural bodies. Directly below Leibniz pluralizes *Li*, which should cause some discomfort to sinologists. In his review of the Loosen–Vonessen German translation of the *Discourse*, Zempliner argues that these passages show that for Leibniz, *li* = monads (p. 228). See also fns. 43, 110.

[42] Although Leibniz underlines here, he is paraphrasing Longobardi on Zhu Xi and not quoting directly.

[43] As in this context, Leibniz usually invoked the celebrated doctrine of pre-established harmony in conjunction with the mind-body problem. Leibniz sees the Chinese facing the same difficulty as

intention is not at all to make the Li's or Spirits (and much less the Li absolutely or principally) material.[44] He is far from this since he has just distinguished between air and the Spirits which animate it. Nor does he say that the Li is the matter of things but seems to suggest that the individual Li's are more or less perfect emanations (according to their organs) of the great Li. Consequently the differences of things are proportionate to the subtlety and the extension of their matter, since their Li's themselves correspond to them. In this he says nothing which is not true.

§15   However, having provided explicit passages from the Chinese classical authors which make the Li the source of perfection, Father Longobardi cites none which show it to be the formless prime matter of the Scholastics, which he claims to prove by reasoning; but his reasoning is not as clear as the explicit [Chinese] passages. Here are his reasons (14:79) which I find very weak: (1) He says that Li cannot subsist by itself and has need of primal air.[45] I do not know if the Chinese say that explicitly.

---

the rationalists (e.g., the Cartesians) of his day, namely how to explain the interaction of "immaterial qualities" and "material particles," or more specifically, of a soul with its own body, given that each is a totally different substance with no common attributes. Since he has already rejected the alternative of strict materialism for the Chinese, and finds Descartes's answer unintelligible, Leibniz believes:

> There remains only my hypothesis, that is to say, the *way of pre-established harmony*—
> pre-established, that is, by a Divine, anticipatory artifice, which so formed each of these
> substances from the beginning, that in merely following its own laws, which it received with its
> being, it is yet in accord with the other, just as if they mutually influenced one another. . . .

(*New System, and Explanation of the New System;* Parkinson, p. 131). Further, *all* substances (and not just an individual soul and its body) are created and preformed with certain natural dispositions or propensities (see §18), which they will actualize naturally in time and in keeping with the pre-established harmony that God ordained from the beginning. This perfectly timed and executed correlation of all substances not only solves the mind-body problem for Leibniz, but also affords a satisfactory explanation without resorting to "influxes" or other invisible or miraculous causal agencies. This "organic philosophy" is similar in many respects to the metaphysics of the Neo-Confucians. See the Introduction, pp. 2–3.

[44] Leibniz is here laying groundwork for the argument he will develop in §23.

[45] "Primal air" is *qi*. The French is *primogène*, meaning "first generated or produced [air]." Elsewhere Leibniz uses *protogène* in the same way.

Perhaps they would say that it cannot act by itself because it naturally acts in things, since it produces things only by means of prime matter by which they apparently mean this primal air. Hence he has only demonstrated thus far that the Li is not prime matter.

§16 His second reason is that according to the Chinese, the Li, considered in itself, is inanimate, without life, without design and without intelligence. Elsewhere the Father records views which confirm this. The universal cause, he says (5:32), according to the Chinese scholars, has neither life nor knowledge nor any other power; they say the same of Heaven, where the Li manifests itself most clearly. The Father cites the Xu-King (11:54; one of the earliest of Chinese works), Book I, p. 33, where it is said that Heaven, which is the most significant thing of the world, neither sees, nor understands, nor hates, nor loves.[46] He also cites the Chinese [Hsing-li] Philosophy, Book 26, pp. 16–17, where it is said that Heaven and Earth have neither reason, will nor deliberation. And Father de Sainte-Marie (p. 81), following Father Ricci, cites the Lung-iu, Chapter 14, where in explicating the Li as the Tao (order), Confucius says that it is incapable of knowing man, but man is capable of knowing it.[47] One must, however, have a very exact translation of this passage in order to see if Confucius speaks there of the first principle, or whether he is not speaking of law or order in abstracto as when one also says among us that the law knows no one, that is, it has no regard for the individual before it.

§16a In addition, I answer that if the classical Chinese authors deny to the Li, or first principle, life, knowledge and power, they mean without

---

[46] The reference here must be to the *Shu Jing*, Part II, Book II, 7, which Leibniz also cites below (see fn. 53). Legge (vol. III, p. 74) translates the passage so that it flatly contradicts Longobardi's: "Heaven hears and sees as our people hear and see; Heaven brightly approves and displays its terrors, as our people brightly approve and would awe. . . ." The thrust of Confucian thought on this issue, however, is much better captured by Karlgren's translation of the same passage: "Heaven's seeing and hearing (proceed from) work through our people's hearing and seeing, Heaven's (enlightenment) discernment and (fearsomeness) severity work through our people's discernment and severity (sc. against bad rulers)." (See Karlgren [2], p. 9) That is, the will of Heaven is expressed, and known, through human deeds.

[47] The reference is to *Lun Yu* 15:28, which reads *ren neng hong dao, fei dao hong ren* 人 能 弘 道 非 道 弘 人 . The term "hong" does not mean "know," and the translation should read: "Men can enlarge *Dao*; *Dao* cannot enlarge men."

doubt these things ἀνθρωποπαθῶς[48] in human form and as they exist among created beings. By life, they would mean the animation of organs; by knowledge the knowledge which is acquired by reasoning or experience; and by power they would mean the power such as that of a prince or magistrate who governs his subjects only by awe and by hope.[49]

§16b   However, in ascribing to the Li the greatest perfections, they ascribe to it something more exalted than all this, of which the life, knowledge and power of creatures are only shadows or feeble imitations. It is somewhat like those mystics—among others Dionysius the Pseudo-Areopagite—who have denied that God could be a Being, ens, ὢν, but have said at the same time that he could be greater than being, super-ens, ὑπερουσία.[50] Thus do I understand the Chinese, who say, according to Father de Sainte-Marie (p. 62), that the Li is the law which governs, and the intelligence which guides things; that it is, however, not itself intelligent, but through natural force, its operations are so well regulated and sure, that one could say that it is intelligent. In our way of speaking, where one must seek and deliberate in order to act properly, we would say that the Li is more than intelligent; whereas for the Chinese it is infallible by its very nature. As for Heaven and Earth, perhaps the author, in speaking of them, believed that they truly lack knowledge (which we believe too), although they are governed by knowledge, reason and order.

---

[48] "as human qualities." Leibniz is alluding here to the *via negativa* or "negative way" (usually associated with mystical theology), which claims that since God is infinite and transcendent, we cannot ascribe—but indeed must explicitly negate—any predicates (e.g., life, knowledge, power) that are associated with finite, created beings. Thus God may only be described by denying Him any characteristic that implies such finitude. Indeed, the use of the word "infinite" is the best example of such an approach. See also fn. 50 below.

[49] Leibniz is referring back to Longobardi here, and the latter was using, in this context, "life," "knowledge," and "power" as his own terms, not as translations from the Chinese.

[50] "above being." Virtually nothing is known about Pseudo-Dionysius, as he is more often called, except that his writings were first cited in the sixth century and that he was clearly a devout Christian who had absorbed the traditions of late Neo-Platonism concerning the "negative way" of describing God (see fn. 53) even more strongly than the later mystics such as Nicholas of Cusa. Pseudo-Dionysius claims that one cannot even say that God "exists" or has "Being." Although the "Cause and Origin and Being and Life of all creatures," (*The Divine Names*, I, 3) "[God] Itself exists not, for It is beyond all Being." (*Ibid.*, I, 1.) See Rolt.

§17   The third argument [of Longarbardi's] is that the L̲i̲ acts only contingently and not by will or deliberation. From the L̲i̲ (5:33), the (primal) air[51] is emitted naturally and contingently; equally naturally and contingently (34) the agitated air produced heat, and (36) consequently the creation of Heaven and Earth occurred purely contingently in a manner quite natural, i.e., with neither deliberation nor design. He also says (11:54) that Heaven and Earth act only by natural propensity, just as fire burns and stones fall. Further (14:77) the L̲i̲ is the natural law of Heaven and by its operation all things are governed, according to weight and measure, and conforming to their state; not, however, on the basis of intelligence or reflection, but only by propensity and natural order. The governance (17:88) and the order of things of this world stems naturally and necessarily from the L̲i̲, following the connectedness of all things, and the disposition of individual subjects, which we call destiny. The same Father says (17:90), I asked a celebrated man, leader of a school with a great number of disciples, who understood perfectly the doctrine of the three sects (that is, the literati, the bonzes or the idolators, and the Tao-cu, which the Europeans call sorcerers),[52] I asked him (I said) if the King-on-high (X̲angti the Lord of Heaven) had life and intelligence, if he knew the good and evil which men do, and if he rewarded and punished them. The response of this learned man is noteworthy. He responded that the King-on-high had none of this knowledge but acted as if he had, thus conforming to what is said in the Xu-King, Book I, p. 35, that Heaven neither sees nor understands nor loves nor hates, but performs all these operations through the efforts of . . . the people . . . with whom the L̲i̲ is connected.[53]

---

[51] See fn. 45.

[52] "Doctrine" is in the singular in both Longobardi and Leibniz, so the reference may be to the syncretist movements. The parenthetical remark, however, suggests the three schools separately: the Confucians, Buddhists, and Daoists respectively.

[53] The Longobardi text is ambiguous about who is quoting whom with respect to the *Shu Jing.* "For Heaven neither loving nor hating, etc.," see fn. 51. Leibniz, however, cites p. 35 for this quote, whereas he earlier cites p. 33. The *Shu Jing* does make reference to Heaven (*tian*) and Lord-on-high (*Shang di*) in the Book following the last one cited. The gist of the passage is that if the ruler is virtuous, and appoints only virtuous officials, the people will respond, showing that the ruler has the support of the Lord-on-high, and that Heaven's mandate will remain with him. Legge, vol. III, p. 79, and Karlgren (2), p. 11. Again, in neither passage does *Li* occur.

§18 All these expressions of the Chinese have a rational meaning. They say of Heaven what we say of the beasts, namely that they act according to intelligence and as if they possessed it, although they do not possess it at all because they are directed by the supreme order of reason; which the Chinese call Li. When they say that the primal air or matter leaves the Li naturally and involuntarily, it could be they believe that God has created matter necessarily. But one could grant yet a better meaning to their words, explaining them more fittingly: namely, that supreme Reason has been brought to that which is the most rational. It is possible they call the Li necessary, because it is determined and infallible; misusing the term "necessary" as many Europeans do.[54] And they have excluded voluntary action because they have understood by voluntary, an act of design and deliberation where at first one is uncertain and then one makes up one's mind afterwards—something which has no place in God. Thus I believe that without doing violence to the ancient doctrine of the Chinese, one can say that the Li has been brought by the perfection of its nature to choose, from several possibilities, the most appropriate; and that by this means it has produced the Ki or matter[55] with dispositions such that all the rest has come about by natural propensities, in the same way that Monsieur Descartes claims to bring forth the present order of the world as a consequence of a small number of initially generated assumptions. Thus the Chinese, far from being blameworthy, merit praise for their idea of things being created by their natural propensity and by a pre-established harmony.[56] But contingency [as Longobardi uses it in his third argument] is not at all appropriate here and does not appear to be based in any way on the words of the Chinese.

§19 The fourth objection of Father Longobardi is based on a false supposition: he says that the Li is the subject of all generation and of all corruption, taking on or discarding various qualities or accidental forms. But there is nothing in the passages that he quotes which says this of the Li, or rule, or supreme Reason. They speak rather of the primal air, or of

---

[54] This is not an example of Leibniz's best argumentative style. No expression in ancient Chinese approximates the meaning of "necessary" as used in Western philosophy and religion. Thus his "It is possible they call the Li necessary, misusing the term, . . ." should not be credited.

[55] See fn. 45.

[56] See fn. 43.

matter, through which the Li creates the primitive entelechies or the substantive operating qualities, which form the constitutive principle of spirits.[57]

§20 His fifth objection is also based on a false or mistaken supposition: namely, that according to the Chinese all things of the world are necessarily material and that there is nothing truly spiritual. As proof of this he cites Books 26 and 34 of their [Xing li] Philosophy. He would have done well, however, to give us the passages concerning this point. But I believe (as I have already said)[58] that the Chinese recognize no distinct immaterial substance other than the Li which has produced Matter. In this I believe they are correct and that the order of things brings it about that all individual Spirits are always united to bodies and that the soul, even after death, is never stripped of all organized matter or of all informed air.[59]

§21 Father Longobardi relies heavily on the Chinese axiom which says that all things are one. He mentions it expressly (7:41) and returns to it often.[60] Father de Sainte-Marie also speaks of it (p. 72).[61] There is yet another passage recorded by Father de Sainte-Marie (p. 73) which shows that there exists something more than material qualities. The Sing-Li Philosophy, Book 26, p. 8, says that the directing and procreating virtue is not found in the disposition of things and does not depend on them but is composed of and resides in the Li which has dominion over, governs, and produces all. Parmenides and Melissus spoke in the same way but the sense which Aristotle gives them appears different from the sense given to Parmenides by Plato.[62] Spinoza reduces all to a single substance, of which

---

[57] See fn. 41.

[58] In §2.

[59] See fn. 5

[60] And according to Longobardi via Ruiz, the Chinese may have learned this doctrine from Zoroaster (7:41). Cf. *Remarks* §9.

[61] Ste.-Marie translates the saying Van-vote-ie-ti-Van-voe-ie-li (*Wan wu yi di, wan wu yi li*) 萬 物 一 商 萬 物 一 理 , without citation. On "Sing-Li," see fn. 116 below.

[62] Leibniz introduces the references to these specific Greek philosophers because Longobardi has done so in the same passage from which Leibniz has just quoted. Aristotle interprets Parmenides as allowing for an efficient cause (i.e., of motion and attraction) as well as a material one, thus diluting the strict interpretation of the Eleatics that all is one and unchangeable (*Metaphysics*, Book I, Chap. 3, 984b 2–4; 30–31). Plato, on the other hand, adheres to a stricter interpretation of Eleatic

all things are only modifications. It is not easy to explain how the Chinese understand it but I believe that nothing prevents according them a rational interpretation. With respect to that which is passive in them, all things are composed of the same prime matter, which differs only by the forms which motion gives it. Also, all things are active and possess Entelechies, Spirits and Souls[63] only by virtue of the participation of the Li, i.e., the same originative Spirit (God), which gives them all their perfections. And matter itself is only a production of this same primary cause. Thus everything emanates from it as from a central point. But it does not follow from this that all things are different only by virtue of accidental qualities: as, for example, the Epicureans and other materialists believed, admitting only matter, figure and movement, which would truly lead to the destruction of immaterial substances, or Entelechies, Souls and Spirits.

§22   The saying that all is one should be counterposed with another, that the one is all, of which we have spoken above in recounting the attributes of the Li.[64] It means that God is everything by eminence (eminenter), as the perfections of effects are in their cause, and not formally [*formaliter*], as if God was the mass of all things. In the same way, all things are one, but not formally as if they comprised one, or as if this great One were their matter. Rather all things are one by emanation (emanenter), because they are the immediate effects of Him; that is, He attends to them intimately and fully, and expresses Himself in the perfections which He communicates to them according to their degree of receptivity.[65] And it is thus that one says Jovis omnia plena;[66] that He fills

---

monism, including Parmenides, which denies the existence of motion or genuine plurality (*Theatetus* 180E; *Parmenides*, 137CD).

[63] See fn. 41.

[64] I.e., in §4 through §8. Longobardi does not say "one is all"; Ste-Marie and Leibniz use the expression. On "eminenter" and "formaliter," see fn. 17.

[65] The Stoics thought of reason as the creative fire (*Pneuma*) or soul residing in the individual as well as the world at large. God (or Zeus) is often thought of as being the animating force or soul of the world, the latter thus being a gigantic rational animal. In his correspondence with Clarke (Fifth paper, §43), Leibniz makes the same point in criticizing the notion that space is a property of God, thus in effect giving Him divisible parts. "This *God with parts* will be very like the Stoic God, who was the whole universe, considered as a divine animal." (Parkinson, p. 230). See also, "Letter to Hansch" (25 July 1707) Loemker, p. 594.

[66] "Jupiter fills the universe," a phrase taken from Virgil's *Eclogues*, III, 60.

all, that He is in all things and that also all things are in Him. He is at the same time the center and the space because He is a circle of which the center is everywhere, as we have said above.[67] This sense of the axiom "that all is one" is all the more certain for the Chinese, since they attribute to the Li a perfect unity incapable of division—according to the report of Father Longobardi noted above—and what makes the Li incapable of division is that it can have no parts.[68]

§23   One could perhaps claim that in fact the Li cannot be equated with the prime Matter of our philosophers, but that one can conceive of it as the prime form, that is, as the Soul of the World, of which the individual souls would only be modifications. This would follow the opinions of several ancients, the opinions of the Averroists, and in a certain sense, even the opinions of Spinoza, for all of whom secondary matters are only modifications of prime matter.[69] And consequently the supposed individual soul would be no more than those organs through which the Soul of the World operates. This doctrine is not at all tenable, because each soul has its own self or individuality.[70] Individual matter is able to result from modifications of prime matter because prime matter has parts. But prime form or pure activity has no parts; thus secondary forms are not produced *from* the prime one, but *by* the prime one.[71] I do not want to deny that several Chinese may have fallen into this error, but it does not seem to me that the error can be found in the passages of their ancient writers.[72] Father Longobardi, who has spoken to many Mandarins trying to find passages contrary to our theology, would have cited some of them had he found them. Consequently I believe that one can claim [on behalf of the Chinese], without doing violence to their classical authors, that there are

---

[67] See fn. 23.

[68] See §6 and §14.

[69] See fn. 27.

[70] For Leibniz, prime matter itself is not genuinely substance (fn. 27) but gains its existence and identity as an individual substance only when it is informed with a form or soul. Hence for Leibniz, as for many Scholastics, individual identity is based on the particular form of a substance, not its individual or secondary matter, which is simply a modification of prime matter.

[71] See fn. 44. Translators' emphasis.

[72] Among those whom Leibniz believed fell "into this error" was probably Zhu Xi, cited on this point in §14. The error will not be found in the "ancient writers"—i.e., in the classical texts— because discussions about primary and secondary matter do not occur there.

Spirits such as those of Man or Genii which are of difference substances than the L<u>i</u>, although they emanate from it.

[II. *Chinese Opinion Concerning the Productions of God or of the First Principle, Matter, and Spirits*]

§24   Having spoken enough concerning the L<u>i</u>, let us turn to what it produces, following what Father Longobardi tells us from the Chinese authors. From the Li issues the air (5:39), the primitive air (11:49), or the primogeneous (or protogeneous) air (14:79). He calls this primitive air K<u>i</u> (10:48 and 11:56/57); it is the instrument of the L<u>i</u> (11:50). The operations of the Spirits pertain ultimately to the L<u>i</u>, instrumentally to the K<u>i</u>, and formally to the Spirits (11:56). It seems that this K<u>i</u>, or this primitive air, truly corresponds to Matter, just as it corresponds to the instrument of the first principle which moves matter; just as an artisan moves his instrument, producing things. This K<u>i</u> is called air, and for us could be called A<u>ether</u> because matter in its original form is completely fluid, without bonds or solidarity, without any interstices and without limits which could distinguish parts of it one from the other. In sum, this matter [*Ki*] is the most subtle one can imagine.

§24a   Now Father Longobardi expressly states that this K<u>i</u> is a production of the L<u>i</u>. But he also says (5:33) that from the L<u>i</u> the primitive air has naturally issued and (11:56) although the L<u>i</u> performs no operations itself, it commences to do so <u>after having produced its</u> K<u>i</u>, that is, its primitive Air. Now we must indeed overlook the inconsistency into which the good Father has fallen inadvertently. How can one say that the L<u>i</u> does nothing itself, without the K<u>i</u>, if it produces the K<u>i</u>? Can one create without acting? And since the Ki is only the instrument, isn't it necessary to say that its virtue or its principal efficient cause is in the L<u>i</u>? In consequence of this production of prime Matter by the primary principle, or primitive Form, by pure Activity, by the operation of God, Chinese philosophy more closely approaches Christian theology than the philosophy of the ancient Greeks who considered matter as coeval with God, a principle which produces nothing but only informs it. Admittedly, it appears that the Chinese believed that the L<u>i</u> first and always produced its K<u>i</u> and that therefore one is as eternal as the other. But there should be nothing surprising about this since they were apparently ignorant of the one Revelation which can explain to us the beginning of the universe—St. Thomas [Aquinas] and other great doctors having claimed that this dogma could not be demonstrated by reason alone. However, although the ancient Chinese expressly state that the Ki never perishes, they do not explicitly state that it has no beginning.[73] And there are those who believed that because the beginnings of the Chinese empire occurred during the time of the Patriarchs, they could have learned about the creation of the world from them.[74]

§25   It seems that after the Li and Ki comes the Taikie, but Father Longobardi has not written enough about the latter to give us a distinct idea of it.[75] One could almost say that the Taikie is nothing other than the Li working on the Ki: *Spiritus domini qui ferebatur super Aquas*,[76] taking the supreme spirit for the Li, and the waters for the primary fluid—i.e., protogeneous air or Ki or prime matter. Thus the Li and Taikie would not be different things but one and the same thing considered under different predicates. The Father says (5:33) that the Li becomes an infinite globe (this is doubtlessly metaphorical) which they name the Taikie—that which has attained the ultimate degree of perfection and consummation— because it operates effectively and exercises its virtue in the production of things, and gives them that ability which includes pre-established order by virtue of which everything proceeds thereafter by its own natural propensity. Consequently, after creating natural objects God needs only thereafter to proceed in his ordinary course.[77] This is why it seems to me that the

---

[73] Like *li, qi* is not used in a metaphysical sense in classical Confucianism, guaranteeing the truth of Leibniz's ". . . they do not explicitly state . . ." Again, cf. *Remarks* §5–§8.

[74] Prominent among those who so believed was Bouvet, who communicated this view to Leibniz in some detail in his letter of 4 November 1701. (Widmaier [2], pp. 147–169). After referring to Fu Xi as "the prince of all the philosophers," Bouvet went on to add that such a description was not an "atrocious offense against Europe," because Fu Xi was not Chinese, but either Zoroaster, Hermes Trismegistus, or Enoch. Leibniz repeats this idea of the Patriarchs visiting China in §32 and §37. He also referred to it in other correspondence, cited by Merkel, pp. 84–85. Longobardi held a similar view (see fn. 60), and Ste.-Marie suggests in the *Mission Treatise* (p. 21) that the Chinese are descendants of Noah. For more on linking Hebrew scriptures with ancient China among seventeenth century Europeans, see Walker.

[75] Longobardi did discuss *tai ji* in some detail; Section 13 is devoted to it. See also fn. 22.

[76] A slight paraphrase of the Latin vulgate edition of the Bible, Genesis 1:2, "The Spirit of the Lord who is borne upon the waters."

[77] See fn. 43.

Father is somewhat confused (10:47) by confounding the Ki with the Taikie and saying that the Taikie is the primogeneous air.

§25a Perhaps some Chinese assume that a primitive composite has resulted from the primitive form, or Li, and from the primitive matter or Ki; a substance of which the Li is the soul and the Ki its matter. They could comprehend this substance under the name of Taikie, and the entire world would thus be conceived of as an animal, life universal, supreme spirit, a grand personage; the Stoics speak of the world in this fashion. Among the parts of this grand and total animal would be the individual animals just as for us animalcula enter into the composition of the bodies of large animals. But since one does not find this error explicitly in the ancient Chinese authors, it should never be attributed to them, all the more so since they have conceived of matter as a production of God. God will not combine substance with matter, and thus the world will not be an animated being, but rather God will be an intelligentia supramundana; and matter, being only an effect of His, will never be coeval with Him. When Father Longobardi (11:49) says that the Taikie contains within itself the Li and the primitive air or Ki, one should not understand this to mean that it is composed of them but simply that it contains them, as conclusions are contained in their assumptions, because the Taikie is the Li operating on the Ki and thus the Ki is assumed.

§26 One may also attribute to the Taikie the attributes of the Li. It is said (11:53) that all the spirits issue from the Taikie, that the Xangti is the son of the Taikie—as a modern Mandarin said—although one could perhaps be sustained by the ancients in supporting the view that the Xangti is also nothing other than the Li or Taikie conceived as the governing principle of the universe, that is, Heaven; as I will shortly demonstrate. Longobardi says (11:54) that the Spirits are the same Li or the same Taikie, applied to different subjects, such as to Heaven, to Earth and to the Mountains. The latter point is not in accord with what the Mandarin said, however, for if the Xangti or the Spirit of Heaven, is the son of the Taikie, it is not identical with it. But sufficient to say here that the Taikie is equated with the Li; we will see below what can be said of the Xangti. Father Longobardi expresses the title of his 13th section in these terms, viz., that all the Gods of the Chinese, or all the Spirits to which they attribute the governance of things, reduce themselves to only one, which is the Li or Taikie. Though it would be better to do so, I am not going to examine this notion at present, but simply note that [even for Longobardi] the Li and

Taikie can be taken for the same thing. He says, in this section (13:68), that
the Li is the "cause of understanding and the guiding norm of all
nature";[78] but that the Taikie is "nature's womb, containing in itself,
potentially, all possible things."[79] Now he also states the latter of the Li in
14:75 and consequently he is certain (13:68) that the difference between
the Li and the Taikie is only a formality in that the Li denotes an absolute
Being, while the Taikie denotes a Being with respect to things of which it is
the root and origin. He cites Book 26 of the Chinese Philosophy, page 8,
where it is said that causes act incessantly because the Li or the Taikie is
within, governing them and directing them. And in Book One of the same
text, page 31, it says that the Li (Reason) has dominion over the things of
the world and consequently lacks nothing. Book 36, page 9 states that the
Taikie is the cause of the beginning and the end of this world[80] and after a
world is ended it produces another (5:36)—after the revolution of the
great year called *Ta Sui*[81] (4:32)—but that it itself never ends. This proves
that the Taikie is not the world. Finally, according to Ste.-Marie (p. 69), the
Chinese recognize nothing greater nor grander than the Li or the Taikie.
They also [according to Longobardi] say that all things are the same
Taikie. I believe this is not to be understood as if things are parts or
modifications of the Taikie, because their absolute realities or perfections
are emanations of it. But, just as we still often speak in a figurative way as if
souls were particles of divinity, it should not then be surprising if the
Chinese speak of them sometimes in the same manner. And it is in this
sense that the Chinese Philosophy says in Book 26, page 1, that the Li is
one, but that its parts are several. For to speak properly, a thing composed
of parts is never truly One. It is unitary only by external denomination, as
one pile of sand or one army. Thus the first principle does not have any
parts—as other passages already cited have shown.

§27   Father de Sainte-Marie records passages (p. 64) from the Chi-

---

[78] This and the following sentence which Leibniz quotes were written in Latin by Longobardi:
Mentis ratio et totius naturae regula directrix.

[79] *Sinus naturae continens in se virtualiter omnia possibilia.*

[80] Longobardi's text reads "production and destruction" rather than "beginning and end."

[81] *Da cui* 大 歲 , "Great year." The term denotes different time periods—weeks, months, and
so on—and is also a name for the planet Jupiter. Thus the time period alluded to here is almost
surely twelve years. Leibniz's citation should read 5:32 instead of 4:32.

nese where they seem to make up a word Li-Taikie. This word signifies (p. 69), according to Confucius (in the *Chung-Jung*, one of the four Books) substantial truth, Law, the principle and end of all things;[82] there is nothing which does not receive from this its effective and true being, without the essence of any of these things having a single atom of imperfection. It is somewhat like (the Father adds) what we read in Genesis [1:31]: God saw all that he had made and all was good. However, he then (p. 107/108) cites a passage from Lactantius concerning the first principle, where this author, after having cited the ancient poets and philosophers, says that all these opinions, although uncertain, establish providence under the names of Nature, Heaven, Reason, Spirit, Fate, Divine Law, which all amount to what we call God.[83] Father de Sainte-Marie then adds that the Chinese recognize only a material principle divided into small parts. In this it seems to me that the good Father is being misled by a strange prejudice which comes to him not from classical authors but from the discourses of some modern impious ones who, in China as elsewhere, see themselves as free thinkers in order to set themselves above the people.

§28   What the Chinese speak of as the most magnificent after the Li or the Taikie is the Xangti, that is, the King-on-high, or rather the Spirit which governs Heaven. Having come to China and remaining there for some time, Father Ricci believed that one could take this Xangti to mean the Lord of Heaven and Earth; in a word our God, Whom he also called Tien-chu,[84] the Lord of Heaven. In China, it is by this last term that one usually refers to the God of the Christians. Fathers Longobardi, S.-Marie and others who do not sanction calling God Xangti are satisfied with the

---

[82] This sentence follows Leibniz's text, but Ste.-Marie does not imply that the Chinese "made up" a word for *li/tai ji* in the *Zhong Yong*. Again, philosophical *li* does not occur in this classical text; rather does the philosophically significant term *dao* 道 "Way"—occur, and the later Neo-Confucian philosophers interpreted *dao* as signifying *li* in the ancient writings. Ste.-Marie says that for *him* the two expressions have the same meaning. They probably did for Longobardi as well; see his commentary on the *Zhong Yong* in (14:77).

[83] *The Divine Institutes,* Book I, Ch. 5.

[84] *Tian Zhu* 天 主 , "Heaven's Lord." This was Ricci's term for "God," although he was willing to allow the ancient Chinese terms *tian* and *Shang di* to be translated in the same way. After the conclusion of the "Terms Controversy," only *Tian Zhu* could be used by the Catholic missionary translators for "God."

name Tien-chu, although in effect the two terms signify almost the same thing in Chinese—keeping in mind the force of the terms "King-on-high" and "Lord of Heaven." The main question is, whether the Xangti is an eternal Substance or a mere creature for the Chinese. Father Longobardi admits (2:13) that the text (from the original books) seems to say that there is a royal sovereign named Xangti who lives in the palace of Heaven from which he governs the world, rewards the good and punishes the wicked. But (on the same page) the same Father contrasts the views of other ancient interpreters who attribute these same qualities to Heaven, or to the universal substance called Li. But far from being detrimental to those who give the name of Xangti to our God, the term serves them marvelously. For the Li is eternal and endowed with all possible perfections; in a word one can take it for our God, as I have shown above. Thus if the Xangti and the Li are the same thing,[85] one has every reason to give to God the name of Xangti. And Father Ricci was not wrong to claim (Longobardi 16:84) that the ancient philosophers of China recognized and honored a supreme being called Xangti, King-on-high, as well as subordinate Spirits—his ministers—and that in this way, they had a knowledge of the true God.[86]

§29   The Chinese say yet other great and good things of Heaven, of the Spirit of Heaven, of the order of Heaven, all of which are most fittingly said of the true God. For example, they say (17:99) the order of Heaven is the being of sovereign goodness which is imperceptible. And they call the Li (14:77) the natural order of Heaven, insofar as all things are governed by weight and measure and conform to their condition [through the operation of the Li]. This order of Heaven is called Tien-tao,[87] and according to Father de Sainte-Marie (p. 69), Confucius in the Chung-Jung says that the Tien-tao is the same as the Li, the determinate order of Heaven in its course and its natural operations.[88] Consequently, according

---

[85] This is Longobardi's claim.

[86] Bouvet went further; according to him, the ancient Chinese, through the Patriarchs, had a knowledge not only of the true God, but of His triune nature as well. See also fn. 74.

[87] *Tian dao* 天 道 , "Heaven's Way."

[88] Again, Leibniz appears to have misread Ste.-Marie's text here, which reads: "Confucius, in the same place, speaking of the Tian dao which is the same as the Li . . ." Ste.-Marie thus makes the two Chinese terms synonymous, but does not ascribe this view to Confucius. See also fn. 82. In the following sentence, the citation to Longobardi should instead read (14:74).

to the account of Father Longobardi (15:81), the universal or primitive substance qua the state it possesses in Heaven is called Li (that is to say, order or reason). And the Li (14:76) is called an object in Heaven because the first principle, although it is present in all objects of the world, is itself primarily in Heaven—which is the most excellent object of the universe— where its efficacy is most apparent. And in Book 2, Chapter 5 of the *Lun-Ju*,[89] it is said of the Li that this principle is of an incomparable essence that there is nothing equal to it. So too the same praises are given to Heaven, and therefore these praises can be reasonably understood as being given not to matter, but to the Spirit of Heaven or the King-on-high. So must Father de Sainte-Marie be understood when he says (p. 13) that the absolute and supreme divinity of the Chinese literati is Heaven.[90]

§30   Here is how Father de Sainte-Marie quotes a Chinese doctor in speaking of the Xangti (p. 74): "Our Chinese philosophers, examining with great care the nature of Heaven and Earth and all things of the world, recognized that they were all good and that the Li was capable of containing them all, without exception, and that from the grandest to the smallest they possessed the same nature and the same substance, from which we conclude that the Lord or God Xangti is present in each thing, with which it is really one. For this reason, we should preach to men and exhort them to flee from vice which would dishonor and soil the perfections of the Xangti; to follow his justice, otherwise this would offend sovereign reason and supreme justice; and not to injure any beings because this would outrage the Lord Xangti, soul of all created things." This passage shows that according to its author, the Xangti is the universal substance, sovereignly perfect—ultimately the same as the Li. One cannot sanction, however, the statements of this scholar (apparently modern) who would make the Xangti into the soul of things as if it were of their essence.

---

[89] Because *li* does not occur in the *Lun Yu*, it is difficult to ascertain what Leibniz and Longobardi are citing. *Lun Yu* 2:5 discusses rituals, the Chinese term for which is *li* 禮 homophonous with *li* 理 , "Principle." The homonymy might have confused Longobardi, Ste.-Marie, and/or Leibniz, but it would not have confused any literate Chinese. Moreover, there is no passage in the *Lun Yu* which treats of the "incomparable" nature of the other terms with which *li* was often equated, except possibly for 8:19. Mungello (1) suggests (p. 108) that it is a reference to 5:12, wherein it is said that one of the things Confucius refused to discuss was "Heaven's Way"—i.e., *Tian dao.*

[90] Ste.-Marie then goes on to describe Confucius as the Chinese Minerva.

§31   The ancient sages of China, believing that the people have a need for objects in their cult which strike their imagination, did not want to propose to the public the reverence of the Li or of the Taikie, but rather the adoration of the Xangti, of the Spirit of Heaven, meaning by this name the Li or the Taikie itself, which manifests its power principally [in Heaven].[91] At times the Hebrews also attribute to Heaven that which pertains to God—as for example in the Book of Maccabees[92]—and they have considered God the Lord of Heaven; for this reason, they were called Coelicolae ["heaven-worshippers"] by the Romans: qui/Nil praeter nubes, et coeli numen adorant.[93] Further, Aristophanes, wanting to make Socrates odious and ridiculous in the eyes of the Athenians, makes the people believe that, contemptuous of the Gods of the land, [Socrates] reveres Heaven or the clouds, which the ignorant confound;[94] this can be seen in his comedy *The Clouds*. It is for this reason Father de Sainte-Marie says (p. 72), that the Chinese philosophers, ancient and modern, revere the visible Heaven and sacrifice to it, under the name of King-on-high, Xangti, because the dominant and visible quality of the Li is incomprehensible to the common people. But it would be better to say that the Xangti, or that which the Chinese revere principally, is the Li which governs Heaven, rather than say that it is the material Heaven itself. Further on (pp. 77/78), Father de Sainte-Marie almost says the same thing himself, the thrust of which is that the Chinese no less than the Japanese (instructed doubtlessly by the Chinese) recognize no other God than a first principle (he adds,

---

[91] This is a particularly obscure passage, which does not seem to make sense without the interpolated phrase. Even with it, the translation is tentative.

[92] God is referred to as "Heaven" (OURANÓS) often in the Book of Maccabees. For example: I, 3:19, 4:10, 24, 40, 55; 9:46, 12:15; 16:3; also in II Maccabees: 7:11; 9:20. He is also called "Sovereign in Heaven" or "Sovereign of the Heavens."

[93] The quote is from Juvenal's *Satires*, V, 14, 97: "They worship nought but the clouds and a god of Heaven." There is no evidence that the Romans referred to the Jews as *Coelicolae*. The verb *colere* has two meanings: "to dwell (inhabit)," and "to worship." In the former sense, the Romans used *Coelicolae* to refer to their own gods: "Heaven-dwellers." (We are grateful to Mr. John Tagliabue for the information in this footnote.)

[94] ". . . il adoroit le Ciel, ou les nuages, *ce que les ignorans confondoient*, . . ." Given the plot of *The Clouds*, and the thrust of Aristophanes' attack on Socrates therein, the text should read "which confound the ignorant." But the French phrase which Leibniz underlined above is clearly to be translated as "which the ignorant confound."

without foundation, <u>material</u>); that they call him the supreme king, <u>Xangti</u>, in his capacity as having dominion over Heaven; that Heaven is his Palace; that there on high he leads and governs all and spreads his influence. They sacrifice to this visible Heaven (or rather to its King) and revere in profound silence that <u>Li</u> which they do not name because of the ignorance or the vulgarity of the people who would not understand the nature of the <u>Li</u>. What we call the light of reason in man, they call commandment and law of Heaven. What we call the inner satisfaction of obeying justice and our fear of acting contrary to it, all this is called by the Chinese (and by us as well) inspirations sent by the Xangti (that is, by the true God). To offend Heaven is to act against reason, to ask pardon of Heaven is to reform oneself and to make a sincere return in word and deed in the submission one owes to this very law of reason. For me I find all this quite excellent and quite in accord with <u>natural theology</u>. Far from finding any distorted understanding here, I believe that it is only by strained interpretations and by interpolations that one could find anything to criticize on this point. It is pure Christianity, insofar as it renews the natural law inscribed in our hearts—except for what revelation and grace add to it to improve our nature.

§32   Regarding the Spirit which governs Heaven as the true God, and taking it for the <u>Li</u> itself—that is, for order or for sovereign reason—these ancient sages of China were more nearly accurate than they realized. This is shown by the discoveries of the astronomers that Heaven is the whole known universe and our earth is only one of its subaltern orbs; one can say that there are as many world systems as there are fixed or principal stars, ours being the system of the sun, which is only one of these stars. Thus the governor or Lord of Heaven is the Lord of the Universe. Since however, the Chinese have been fortunate enough to come by this wisdom without sufficient warrant for it, it may be that they learned part of it from the tradition of the Patriarchs.[95]

§33   Let us now see what Father Longobardi offers in contrast on this point. He says (2:18) that according to Chinese scholars, the Xangti is Heaven itself or rather the virtue and the power of Heaven. But to say that the Xangti is the material Heaven is implausible. As for its being the virtue and power of Heaven, it could be nothing other than the virtue and power of the entire universe, since Heaven comprises all that we know of the

---

[95] See fn. 74.

universe. The idea of some kind of individual soul for Heaven, which would be the Xangti, is very unlikely, the expanse of Heaven being so immense. It would make more sense to attribute a soul to each system, or rather to each star, as the Chinese attribute one to the earth. The praises given to the Spirit of Heaven, or to the Order of Heaven, would not be suitable to an individual soul; they are appropriate only to the Li. Thus (11:52) if Ching Cheu, a classical author,[96] has said that the Xangti is the same thing as Heaven, one can take this expression as figurative or as less than exact, just as we often use "Heaven" to denote the Lord in Heaven. It may also be that this author considered Heaven as a person of which the soul is the Li, and of which the body is the celestial material; and consequently he would have regarded Heaven as the Stoics regarded this world. But until such time as one can better examine this passage, it is more plausible to think that he spoke figuratively (as is still customarily done in Europe) in speaking of Heaven as God.

§34   According to Father de S.-Marie (p. 57), ancient Chinese writings contain the following anecdotes: the Emperor Vuen-Wang[97] persevered all his life to be humble and to hide the splendor of his majesty, to rectify himself and to abase himself before this Lord and King-on-High, Xangti. The Emperor named Hia Xi,[98] when he reproached himself for a wicked action, trembled in fear and respect before the Xangti and had the habit of saying that this fear and respect restrained him so that he dared not commit a sin against true reason. In ancient times the Emperor himself cultivated the earth on which the seed offered to the sovereign King and Lord Xangti was sown. Further (p. 59), a King of China asked Confucius if one should pray to the tutelary god of fire or the more inferior one of the

---

[96] Longobardi gives no sources here, and because he is not consistent in his method of transliteration it is not possible to identify "Ching Cheu," which does not occur elsewhere in the *Religion Treatise*. It is possibly the name of an early Neo-Confucian commentator on the classics.

[97] One of the transliterations for King Wen 文 王, founder of the Chou Dynasty (1050–256 B.C.).

[98] Ste-Marie (p. 57) provides no source for the anecdote of "Hia Xi," who is unknown. In the Loosen–Vonessen translation it is plausibly suggested (p. 147) that the reference may be to the *Shu Jing* chapter in which Tang, founder of the Shang Dynasty says: "The Xia sovereigns [*Xia shi* 夏 氏] have offended; and because I fear *Shang di*, I dare not let them go unpunished." (Translation modified from Legge, vol. III, p. 174.) If this suggestion is correct, however, then Ste.-Marie (and thus Leibniz) have attributed the lauded qualities to the wrong person.

hearth. Confucius answered him that if one had given offense to Heaven—that is to the Lord of Heaven—it is from him alone that one should ask pardon.[99] This seems to show that Confucius, like Plato, believed in the unity of God but accommodated himself to popular prejudices.[100]

§34a   Father Longobardi himself recounts (17:90) the conversation which he had with a Chinese doctor, who told him that the King-on-High or Xangti[101] was the same as Heaven, Li, Taikie, Ivan-Ki[102] (the author does not explain this term), the Tien-Xing[103] (or genii, p. 19), the Tien-Ming[104] (virtue sent from Heaven), the Nan-lin[105] (virtue of the earth). The same doctor also said that the Xangti of the literati sect was the Spirit or the God which the Bonzes venerated under the name of Foe[106] and the Tao-cu

---

[99] Ste-Marie provides no source here, but the reference must be to *Lun Yu* 3:13. Only the term *Tian*, "Heaven," occurs therein, however; Ste.-Marie equates it with *Shang di* ("Lord-on-High"), and Leibniz has altered the equation to "Lord of Heaven," which is what is usually used for *Tian zhu*. See fn. 84.

[100] Although most scholars believe, on both theological and etymological grounds, that Plato was not a monotheist, there is nevertheless the statement by Plato himself in Epistle XIII which shows that he could make the distinction between "God" and "gods" if necessary. In writing to Dionysius, Plato says:

> You no doubt recall the sign that distinguishes the letters I write that are seriously intended from those that are not. . . . Those that are seriously meant begin with "God"; those less seriously with "gods." (*Plato's Epistles*, p. 268.)

Leibniz was clearly aware of these letters of Plato. For further details, see Riley, p. 209.

[101] Neither Longobardi nor the Chinese doctor say "Xangti"; Leibniz has added the phrase.

[102] Probably *Yuan qi* 元 氣 , "Primal *qi*." This term is first found in the *Huai Nan Zi* 淮 南 子 , an early metaphysical text of the Former Han Dynasty, written ca. 130 BCE This work is not a part of the Confucian classical corpus, but was widely read.

[103] There are four possibilities here: (1) The term is *Tian-shen* 天 神 , "Heavenly spirits"; (2) Being equated with *li* and *Tai ji*, however, the term could be *Tian xing* 天 行 , "Heaven's conduct," or "Heaven's path"; or it could be (3) the Daoist term *Tian xing* 天 性 , "Heaven's nature." The last possibility would be (4) the Daoist term *Tian xian* 天 仙 , "Heavenly Immortals," suggested by Leibniz's parenthetical remark. See also fn. 112.

[104] *Tian-ming* 天 命 , "Heaven's mandate." See *Preface* §13.

[105] It is not clear what "Nan-lin" refers to; it is not a common Chinese compound. Longobardi translates it as "Husband of the earth," which Leibniz has altered. Nan must be 男 ("male").

[106] *Fo* 佛 , i.e., the Buddha.

under the name of Jo-Hoang.[107] Another has said (17:87) that our heart (that is what operates within us) is the same thing as the Xangti and Tien-Cheu, for the Chinese say that the heart is the Chu Zay[108] (or director) of man, regulating all his physical and moral actions (15:81). This shows how some Chinese often speak vaguely and confusedly under the pretext that all is one, and that one should not always take them literally. To be able to speak clearly of their dogmas, it is safest to consider the reason and the harmony of their doctrines, rather than superficial utterances.

§35 Father Longobardi also recounts the discourse of Chinese Mandarins who told him that the Xangti and the Tien-Cheu, the King-on-high or Lord of Heaven, is only a production of the Taikie and will end like other creatures while the Taikie itself endures (11:53); that the King-on-high or Spirit of Heaven will cease with Heaven (17:89); and that if our God or our Tien-Cheu (Lord of Heaven) were the same as the Xangti, He would cease to exist as well (17:87, 89). But the good Father produces no passage from the ancients which says as much.[109] On the contrary, it would seem that the ancients wanted to revere the Li in the Xangti. These then are only the ideas of moderns, who try to substitute simple material substances for all spiritual substances, much as the Cartesians do with the souls of beasts,[110] and as some ancients in the *Phaedo* insisted, namely, that the soul is nothing other than a harmony, or a congeries of material dispositions, or a mechanical structure.[111] This tends only to destroy religion (as if it were only a political invention) in order to hold the people in check, which is just

---

[107] *Yu-huang* 玉 皇 , the Jade Emperor, highest Daoist deity. See *Remarks*, n. 10.

[108] *Zhu zai* 主宰 , "Supreme ruler."

[109] Because the "ancients" didn't discuss the topic. Longobardi is not citing the classics, but his Chinese contemporary here.

[110] As noted above, (fns. 41,43), Leibniz saw any substance *qua* substance as possessing some sort of soul or "spirit" (entelechy). On the other hand, Descartes and his followers, as strict dualists, thought of beasts or brutes as having no soul or spiritual qualities and therefore no consciousness at all. Animals for Descartes are finely tuned machines or automata (he likens them to watches; *The Passions of the Soul*, Articles VII, XVI), made up only of matter set in motion by the mechanical beat of the heart (*Discourse on Method*, V).

[111] Simmias elaborates the theory that the soul is nothing but an attunement (HARMONIA) of certain material elements of the body. *Phaedo*, 85B–86D. Cebes follows with another materialist argument against the absolute immortality and indestructibility of the soul, claiming that the latter may still "wear out" after many incarnations. *Ibid*, 87B–88C.

what a Chinese doctor said to Longobardi—the same doctor whose discourse, noted earlier, confounded different things on the basis of a poor understanding of the notion that all is one (17:92).

§36   As taken absolutely, the Universal Spirit is called Li or Order; as operative in Creatures it is called Taikie or that which consummates creation and establishes things; as governing Heaven, the principle creation is called Xangti, or King-on-High or Tien-Chu, Lord of Heaven. Having established this, I want now to turn to the genii, or individual, subaltern Spirits. In general, they are called Tien Xin (Longobardi, Preface, p. 6) or Simply Xin (8:44), or rather Kuei-Xin[112] (Ste.-Marie, p. 89). Father Longobardi notes (I:44) that by the word Xin, the Chinese mean pure rising spirits, and by Kuey, impure or descending spirits. But that does not seem an exact interpretation, since Father de S.-Marie (p. 89) quotes the words of Confucius: "Oh, the rare virtues and grand perfections of these celestial spirits Kuei-Xin! Is there any virtue superior to them? One does not see them, but by their actions they are made manifest. One does not hear them, but the marvels which they never cease to effect speak enough."[113] Confucius also says (recorded on p. 91), that we are not able to conceive in what manner the Spirits are so intimately united with us; thus we cannot be hasty in honoring them or serving them or offering them sacrifices, for although their operations are secret and invisible, their benefits are visible, effective and real.[114]

§37   With such clear statements from a classical author, and a most classical work, it seems to me that the missionaries of whom Father de S.-Marie speaks (p. 90) have had good reason to compare the Spirits or the genii to our Angels. Father de S.-Marie recognizes that the Chinese regarded them as subordinate to Xangti, universal and supreme Spirit of Heaven (p. 89), and he compares them (p. 96) with the ministering or inferior gods of the great God of Seneca, and of St. Augustine when he was

---

[112] *Tian-shen* (see fn. 103), "Heavenly Spirits," and *Gui-shen*, "ghosts and spirits; see *De cultu*, fn. 2. Both terms are often used to refer to the human souls (see fn. 153), and Leibniz, taking his cue from Ste.-Marie and Longobardi, distinguishes "subaltern spirits" from human souls more sharply than most Chinese would have done. See §57ff. for Leibniz's treatment of the human soul. "Genii" has been used by many sinologists of the last century as translation for the Daoist *Xian* 仙 , "immortals".

[113] The quotation is from the *Zhong Yong* XVI, 1–3, where it is attributed to Confucius.

[114] *Ibid.*, XVI, 4–5, and XVII, 1–3.

still a Manichean, as recorded in his *Confessions* [Book VII, 7]. These missionaries have thus believed (with good reason, to my mind), that the most ancient Chinese philosophers, and Confucius after them, have had knowledge of the true God and of the celestial Spirits who serve Him, under the names of Xangti and Kuei-Xin. I say this because the ancient Chinese philosophers seem to ascribe to them a particular concern for defending and protecting men, cities, provinces and kingdoms, not as if they were the souls or the substantial forms of these things, but as if they were pilots of vessels—what our philosophers call assisting intelligences and forms. And it is necessary to admit that the words of Confucius and other ancient authors carry the meaning sensu maxime obvio et naturali.[115] There is a great likelihood that these [Chinese] expressions, so close to the great truths of our tradition, have come to the Chinese through the tradition of the ancient Patriarchs.

§38   Father de Sainte-Marie opposes only those interpreters who are called classical, but who are in fact much later. The great Commentary on the original books called Ta-Ziven, and the compendium of philosophy called Sing-Li (1:11)[116] or what Father de Sainte-Marie calls the Taciven Singli were compiled, according to this Father, by royal order over 300 years ago, so that one may consider them as modern. And their authority concerning the true sense of the ancient texts is no greater than the authority of an Accursius or a Bartolus concerning the explanation of the meaning of the Edictum perpetuum of ancient Roman jurisprudence, which one has found today to be often quite removed from these commentators.[117] It is like several views which the Arabs and Scholastics

---

[115] "In a maximally obvious and natural sense." On the Patriarchs, see fn. 74.

[116] The citation (and transliteration) here is to Longobardi, not Ste.-Marie. The former's description of his sources (1:11–12) is not clear, so that Leibniz might well have been confused by the separation of the names *Ta-Ziven* from *Sing-Li,* which together comprise the *Compendium.* At times, Ste.-Marie also reverses the title, calling it the *Taciven Singli.* See Introduction, pp. 30–31. "*Xingli xue*" 性理學 was also the name of one of the groups of Neo-Confucians, whence the *Compendium* received its title. See also Mungello (1).

[117] The form of the *Edictum*—the decree outlining the jurisdictional procedures, which was issued by each ancient Roman magistrate upon entering his office—was finally stabilized about 130 c.e., by the jurist Salvius Julianus at the instigation of the Emperor Hadrian. This *Edictum Perpetuum* ("Perpetual Edict"), alterable only by the Emperor himself, became an object of legal study in the Middle Ages, even though the original text was lost and its contents known only

have ascribed to Aristotle, which are far removed from the true sense which the ancient Greek interpreters gave to him and which modern interpreters have recovered. And I believe myself to have shown what Entelechie means, which the Scholastics scarcely understood.[118]

§39　Thus the authority that Fathers Longobardi and de Sainte-Marie ascribe to Chinese moderns is only a scholastic prejudice. They have judged the later Chinese school as the medieval European school (with which they are preoccupied) would have us judge them, namely to judge the texts of the divine and human Laws and of ancient authors by their own intepretations and commentaries. This is a defect rather common among philosophers, lawyers, moralists and theologians. It is also common among medical doctors, who not yet having a definite school, nor the same regulated language, have gone so far in contempt of the ancients (and are so eager to shake off such a yoke), that they have fallen into arbitrariness, since they have scarcely anything of established fact beyond experience or observations, which themselves are often not too well ascertained. Consequently it seems that medicine has need of being entirely rebuilt on the basis of the authoritative communications of several of its outstanding practitioners, who would re-establish a common language, would distinguish the certain [from the possible], would provisionally assign probabilities to the latter and would discover a sure method of development for the science—but this is said simply in passing.[119]

§39a　The scant authority of the commentators makes it surprising to

---

through commentaries. Both Franciscus Accursius (c. 1182–1260)—last and greatest of the Glossators of the Bologna school of law—and Bartolus of Saxoferrato (1314–1357), teacher of law at Perugia and the most famous of the so-called "Commentators" or "Post-Glossators," dealt with the *Edictum Perpetuum* in their writings. Both were paragons of medieval jurisprudence for later generations, though for Leibniz, they are examples of the inadequacy of medieval legal studies, given the advances in understanding Roman law in his own day.

[118] See fn. 41.

[119] Leibniz often attacked the scientific pretensions of the medicine and jurisprudence of his day. He thought of medicine as an empirical and *inductive* science, but nevertheless hoped that one day, after firmly establishing certain facts through continued observation and experimentation, it might be possible to discover certain rules or laws which would then be the basis of establishing a rational, *deductive* science of medicine. Leibniz was certain that the latter could be done with the principles of law and often attacked those who thought of jurisprudence as based simply on various empirical rules. See Couturat, pp. 154–155.

me that very clever theologians of our time, who prefer the doctrine of the ancient Fathers of the Church to modern sentiment in speculative theory as well as in morality, nevertheless pretend to judge Chinese theology through modern eyes rather than ancient ones. One should not find it at all surprising in a Father Longobardi or in a Father de S.-Marie, who apparently reflect the sentiments of a vulgar theological and philosophical school. But it seems to me that among scholarly theologians who oppose themselves to the Jesuits on this matter of Chinese doctrine, there must be others who should be able to judge quite otherwise.

§40   Father de S.-Marie does record something in passing which could make us suspect that the ancient [Chinese] philosophers did not have true beliefs [i.e., consistent with Christian doctrine]. But since he scarcely dwells on it, I doubt that the matter can be adequately verified or made clear. However, I do not wish to conceal it, so I will proceed with all possible sincerity. After having quoted (p. 89) the fine passage of Confucius noted above, he claims that the same author, continuing his discourse, discovers how far his vulgar error on this point goes. For Confucius says (according to this Father), that the Spirits are in truth united and incorporated with all things, from which they are unable to separate themselves without being totally destroyed.[120] This opinion conforms very much (says the Father) to the overall philosophy of Confucius, in which he teaches that the Nature and essence of things is the Li, Taikie, their first principle and their Creator, which as King of Heaven is called Xangti (that is, Supreme King). That which dominates the individual and subaltern Beings, where generation and corruption take place, is called Kuei-Xin. Now as matter and form cannot be separated without the destruction of the whole unit that they constitute, in the same way, spirits are so united to things, that they could not leave them without their own dissolution.[121]

§41   I wanted to cite word for word the words of Father de S.-Marie which I am now going to examine. I should say at the outset that I am inclined to believe that these are not the express doctrines of Confucius, but opinions which have been ascribed to him on the basis of modern intepretations. For the actual words recorded of him do not bear this meaning, unless one wanted to claim that he spoke under the veil of religion simply to fool his unsophisticated readers. But the charge that his

---

[120] See below, fn. 122.

[121] Leibniz uses this argument in another context in §64.

true beliefs were those of Atheists should only be made on the basis of solid evidence, for which I have seen absolutely no basis until now, other than the veiled interpretations of modern commentators who would probably not dare to assert as much explicitly. If Confucius had this opinion concerning Spirits, he would not have thought any more positively of them than our ordinary Schoolmen do concerning the souls of animals—i.e., they believe them to perish with the animal itself. But if that were so, how is it that Confucius ascribes to these Spirits and Genii those rare virtues and great perfections, those marvelous operations, those grand benefits worthy of our recognition and worship?

§42 Furthermore, Confucius and the ancients ascribe Spirits and ministering genii to several things which are not at all suited for such ascriptions, for example to men, to towns and to provinces. But then, what is the likelihood of a Spirit being incorporated with its mountain, or river, or the likelihood even of the spirit of the four seasons being incorporated with the seasons themselves, or of the spirit of hot and of cold being incorporated with these qualities? Thus it must be said either that these ancient Chinese were hoodwinking the people and sought only to mislead them—a charge one should not make without proof—or that they believed in subaltern spirits, ministering agents of the divinity, each governing matters in his own department; or finally, that they honored, through their names, a divine quality that was suffused everywhere, as some ancient Greeks and Romans claimed that they worshipped only one Godhead, but under the names of several Gods.

§43 Furthermore, I suspect that Father de S.-Marie has mistaken the meaning of Confucius when he interprets the latter as saying that spirits cannot be separated from the things they govern without being destroyed. Confucius seems rather to have said that Spirits cannot separate themselves from things without those things they are meant to govern being destroyed, for this is how I find that Father Longobardi has understood it, citing Chapter 16 of the Chung-Jung (11:57) where Confucius, after having taught that spirits are parts which compose the being of things, adds that Spirits can be separated from them, but only with the destruction of those things (he does not say of the spirits) ensuing.[122] Further, there is the

---

[122] Leibniz is following Longobardi's text, but they both read too much into the *Zhong Yong* passage, which reads: 體 物 而 不 可 遺 . "[The *gui-shen*] are present in things, and may not leave them." Ste.-Marie (fn. 120) must have been referring to the same passage.

likelihood that since Confucius made spirits parts of things, he did not mean all spirits, for the reasons I have cited [in §41 and §42]. Perhaps also the term part is taken here in a broader sense, i.e., as that which is in a thing, and is required for its subsistence of conservation.

§44   There are many Chinese moderns who claim to be followers of Confucius and the ancients, but who do not at all recognize the existence of spiritual substances, and not even of true substances, excepting matter, which they consider as alterable only by figural motions and by accidental qualities. According to these moderns, I say, celestial or other spirits which the ancient Chinese ascribe to things are only nominal, denominating simply the mass of accidental qualities of matter, and are like the forms which make up the Beings *per accidens* of the Schoolman,[123] i.e., a pile of stones, mountains of sand, etc.—forms quite inferior without doubt even to the souls of beasts. Whether one takes these souls in the manner of the Scholastics, or in the Cartesian sense (much better organized, but still a mass of accidental qualities); on either interpretation, these souls are quite removed from meriting worship, since the Spirit of Heaven, the Spirit of natural causes, the Spirit of the mountains (for example) lack organs, and consequently they would be incapable of knowledge and even of the possibility of knowledge. Thus it would be pure deceit to want to do homage to them.

§45   The Xu-King, one of the most ancient and seminal works according to Father Longobardi (1:10), recounts, Chapt. 1, page 11 (11:51), that since the time of Jao and of Xun[124] (early founders of the Empire), the Chinese have revered Spirits and that four kinds of sacrifices were made to four kinds of Spirits. The first sacrifice, called Lui,[125] was made to Heaven and collectively to its Spirit called Xangti. The second, called In,[126] was made to the Spirit of the six principle causes, i.e., the four seasons of the year, heat, and cold, the Sun, the Moon, the stars, the rain and dryness. The third, named Vuang,[127] was made to the Spirit of the

---

[123] As opposed to a Being in itself or *ens per se,* such as an animal with a soul and an organized body. See also fns. 5 and 110.

[124] The legendary sage rulers Yao and Shun 堯 , 舜 , who reigned ca. the twenty-fourth and twenty-third centuries BCE. The *Shu Jing* source is in Legge, vol. II, pp. 33–34.

[125] *Lei* 類 .

[126] *Yin* 禋 .

[127] *Wang* 望 .

Mountains and of the great rivers. And the fourth, named Pien,[128] was made to the Spirits of things of lesser importance in the Universe, and to illustrious men of the empire. Now the same Father notes (2:13) that according to the text, there are different spirits, which he names Kuei, or Xin or jointly Kuey-Xin,[129] which preside over the mountains, the rivers or other things in the lower world. But the [Chinese] interpreters explain these rather as natural causes or qualities which produce certain effects.

§46   These interpreters are correct when they do not accept—as the ignorant people of antiquity did—that Jupiter, or some aerial genie throws thunderbolts, that there are certain greybeards, residing in the mountains and the hollows of the earth who pour out the rivers from their urns; they are correct when they believe that all comes about naturally by virtue of the qualities of matter. However, the Chinese interpreters cited by Longobardi are not correct if they believe that the ancients wanted to show reverence to these brute objects and that they reduced the first principle, the governor of Heaven—or rather the governor of the Universe—to this same condition of a mass of brute qualities, since the wonders of particular things, which know not at all what they are doing, could come only from the wisdom of the first principle. Therefore, one must believe either that the ancient sages of China believed that certain Genii, as Ministers of the supreme Lord of Heaven and Earth, presided over earthly things, or that they still wanted to revere the Great god through the qualities of individual things, under the names of the Spirits of these things, for the benefit of popular imagination. If the second alternative is correct, then it is in this way that they believed that all is one; that the quality of a grand, unique principle appears throughout the wonders of particular things, and that the Spirit of the seasons, the Spirit of the mountains, the spirit of the rivers, was the same Xangti who governs Heaven.

§47   This second alternative is the truest. However, the first view, which acknowledges genii presiding over natural things, celestial spheres, etc., is not at all intolerable to, nor destructive of, Christianity, as I have already remarked above [in §2]. It will be easy to teach and make the Chinese receptive to that which is the most true by a reasonable interpretation of this Axiom that the all reduces itself to the power of the one; that is,

---

[128] *Pian* 偏 .

[129] *Gui-shen.* See fn. 112.

that the powers of all inanimate creatures do not manifest their own wisdom, but the wisdom of the Author of things and they are only a natural consequence of forces which the first principle instills in them. It will be more difficult, however, to make them understand—following the true philosophy of our time—that animated substances are potentially everywhere, but they actually exist only where there are bodies that can perceive;[130] that these animated substances have their own souls or spirits as does man, and that there is an infinity of them above as well as below the Soul or Spirit of man. Moreover those substances which are above are called Angels and *Genii,* some of which, more specifically, serve the supreme Spirit, being more disposed to comprehend his will and conform themselves to it; that the souls of virtuous people are associated with them, rendering the latter worthy of homage, but not to the destruction of one's obligations to the supreme substance.

§48 Thus one can even find satisfaction with modern Chinese interpreters, and commend them, since they reduce the governance of Heaven and other things to natural causes and distance themselves from the ignorance of the masses, who seek out supernatural miracles—or rather super-corporeal ones—as well as seek out Spirits like those of a Deus ex machina. And one will be able to enlighten them further on this matter by acquainting them with the new discoveries of Europe which give virtually mathematical reasons for some of the great wonders of nature, and by acquainting them with the true systems of the Macrocosm and the

---

[130] See §2. The "true philosophy of our time" is, of course, Leibniz's own. He is referring to his theory that there are an infinity of substances or monads that have life, that is, that are informed with souls (*animae*) or entelechies that enable them to feel and/or perceive. There are infinitesimal levels of such feelings or perceptions, each blending into the next (Leibniz's doctrine of *petites perceptions*). Some substances are endowed or "preformed" with bodily organs giving them the potential for apperception or reflective consciousness. Such potentialities are eventually realized in accordance with a preestablished harmony (see §14 and fn. 43); that is, when there is a complete correlation between the level of complexity and subtlety of the matter and the corresponding form or soul. Leibniz believed that this theory was the only one which explained the origin of individual forms or souls without appealing to purely materialistic ground (viz., that the soul *is nothing but* a particular collocation of material atoms) or to God's consistently miraculous and *ad hoc* creation of new forms or souls (see §13). The *Monadology*, §§14ff. and *Theodicy*, §91 give accounts of this central doctrine of Leibniz's mature philosophy.

Microcosm.[131] But at the same time, it is necessary to make them recognize, as reason demands, that these natural causes—which render their functions so exactly at a particular point in order to create many of the wonders [of the world]—could not be brought about were it not for mechanisms prepared for, and formed by, the wisdom and power of the supreme substance, which one may call, with them, Li.

§48a It is for this reason perhaps that Confucius did not want to explain himself concerning the Spirits of natural things;[132] he thought that what should be revered in the Spirit of Heaven, the seasons, the mountains, and other inanimate things was only the supreme spirit, the Xangti, the Taikie, the Li, but did not believe the people at all capable of detaching this Supreme Spirit from the objects which fell under their senses, and therefore he did not want to expound on it. This is why, according to F. Longobardi (3:27), in the Lunxin,[133] Chap. 3, Part 3, a disciple of Confucius named Zuku[134] said as if in complaint of his Master: "I never got him to speak about human nature and the natural state of Heaven, except at the end of his life." In the same book, Confucius says, "The proper way of governing the people is to so act that they honor the Spirits while distancing themselves from them." That is, he refrained from wanting to

---

[131] It is hard to know exactly what specific discoveries Leibniz is referring to concerning the "true systems of the Macrocosm and the Microscosm." The belief that man, the Microcosm, "mirrors the universe" or Macrocosm (and *vice versa* in that both are constructed according to the same proportions or have the same organic structure) is an ancient doctrine with many variations, going back to the pre-Socratics. With his characteristic immodesty, Leibniz is probably alluding to his own doctrine, whereby "every single substance is a perpetual living mirror of the universe" (*Monadology*, §56) and "every monad . . . is representative of the universe from its own point of view, and is as much regulated as the universe itself" (*Principles of Nature and Grace* [1714], §3). The same coherent body of natural laws and the same harmony (see §14, fn. 43) pre-established by God to govern individual substances governs the universe as a whole. In this sense, Leibniz claims, we should understand the Chinese doctrine that "all is one"; that is, "that the quality of a grand, unique principle appears throughout the wonders of particular things" (end of §46 above).

[132] A reference to *Lun Yu* 7:20: "The Master would not discuss unusual occurrences, physical strength, disorder, or spirits [*shen* 神]." See also fn. 37.

[133] The *Lun Yu*. The reference should be 5:12.

[134] Zigong 子貢 (520–450? B.C.E.), one of the most famous disciples of Confucius. In this section Leibniz is quoting Longobardi directly.

examine what the Spirits are and what they do.[135] In Book 4, page 6, it is said that there were four things—Spirit one among them—about which Confucius maintained a great silence.[136] Commentaries state that the reason for this is because there are several matters difficult to understand, and consequently it is unseemly to speak of them to everyone. In the Book Kialu,[137] it is said that Confucius, wanting to deliver himself from the importuning queries of his disciples (who did not cease to question him about the Spirits, the rational Soul and about what happens after death), decided to give them a general rule: to argue and dispute as much as they wanted to on matters concerning the six positions, which are in the visible world (it is necessary to learn more about these six positions); however, with regard to other matters, he desired to leave them be, without discussion and without investigating them more deeply.

§49   From this Father Longobardi (3:28) infers the conclusion that the literati sect possessed an esoteric doctrine reserved for the masters alone; but this does not follow at all, because Confucius himself could have been ignorant about that which he did not want to investigate more deeply. To all appearances there is no such secret sect today in China, unless one would like to say that the Hypocrites[138] constitute one. And even if there were such sects, one cannot rest merely on what people venture to say in

---

[135] *Lun Yu* 6:20. Leibniz has interpolated the phrase "to govern the people." He then inserted, but crossed out, another anecdote from the *Lun Yu*, 11:11. See below, fn. 137.

[136] See fn. 132.

[137] Longobardi provides no source, nor context, for ascertaining the reference of "Kialu." Perhaps it is the *Jia Yu* (家 語)—a text of the Han Confucians—but there is no mention of the "6 positions" in this work. On the other hand, the reference to *Lun Yu* 11:11 that Leibniz crossed out above (fn. 135) concerns one of the disciples of Confucius, Ji-Lu 季 路 (542–479 B.C.), and this chapter fits the context of Leibniz's remarks—except for the "6 positions": "Ji-lu asked about serving the spirits [*gui-shen*]. The Master said, 'Not [yet] being able to serve mankind, how can you serve the spirits?' The disciple then asked about death. The Master said, 'Not [yet] knowing about life, how can you know about death?'" The "6 positions" are the 4 cardinal directions, zenith and nadir.

[138] Like his use of "Atheist Mandarins" in §10 and "free thinkers" in §27, Leibniz probably uses "Hypocrites" here to denote those members of the Chinese intelligentsia of Ming–Qing times who were elaborate but proper in the carrying out of ritual observances and sacrifices, but agnostic, or atheist, in their religious beliefs. See the Introduction, pp. 28–29.

their public works. Everywhere there are some who ridicule their own dogmas. Thus when this Father says (11:58) that the majority of literati acknowledge living spirits or spirits of sacrifice, while prestigious literati acknowledge only spirits of generation and corruption (which are merely simple material properties), I am surprised that the Father wants the Missionaries to pay deference principally to these latter doctors. My own belief is that they should regard them as heterodox, and ally themselves to common, public doctrines.

§50   Furthermore, the Father appears to conclude from the affected silence of Confucius that Confucius himself had wrong opinions. The father says throughout his work that the ancient Chinese were as atheistic as the modern; he says so expressly in section 16, page 84. He believes that this method of Confucius corrupted the hearts and clouded the minds of the Chinese scholars, reducing them to thinking only about visible and palpable matters, and that consequently they fell into the greatest of all evils: Atheism. I would believe that this silence and approach of Confucius contributed to it, and that he would have done better to explain himself further; however, it appears that the moderns have pressed the matter beyond the limits of his method. One could say that far from denying the existence of spirits and of religion, he simply wanted his followers not to dispute about such matters but to content themselves with appreciating the existence and the effects of the Xangti and the Spirits, honoring them and practicing virtue in order to please them, without delving into their nature and without entering into the how or the manner of their operations. Throughout our own history, there have been Christian authors who have given the same advice without having any evil intent. Thus I find that everything that has been said against the ancient Chinese to be only groundless suspicions.

§51   The common authoritative doctrine of the Chinese on Spirits appears sufficiently well presented in a passage of their philosophy which the Father himself recounts (12:61ff.). The Chu-zu,[139] Book 28 of the Great Philosophy, page 2, asks: "Are Spirits made from air?" The answer given is that it appears more likely that they are the force, the power, and the activity in the air, rather than the air itself. On page 13, he [Zhu Xi] distinguishes between good spirits who possess clarity and righteousness

---

[139] Longobardi is quoting a passage written by Zhu Xi—i.e., "Chu-zu"—from the *Compendium*.

and produce good effects in the sun, moon, day, night, etc., on the one hand, and devious and obscure spirits on the other. He adds a third category of spirits who respond to questions asked of them and grant requests made of them.[140] On page 38, he proves that there are spirits by the following reasoning: if there were no spirits, the ancients would not have made demands of them after fasting and other abstinences. Moreover, the Emperor sacrifices to Heaven and Earth; the Princes and Dukes (or heroes) sacrifice to the great rivers and grand mountains; the lords offer five sacrifices, etc.

§52   The same author asks further, "When one sacrifices to Heaven, to Earth, to the mountains and the waters; when one offers up and slaughters [animal] victims; when one burns pieces of silk; when one offers libations of wine; is all this done only in order to demonstrate the heart's good intentions, or indeed because there is an Air (a spirit) which receives the offerings? If we say that nothing comes to receive what is offered, then to whom are we sacrificing? And what is it on high which inspires us with awe and which leads mankind to make sacrifices and to be fearful? If we also say that he descends in a cloud-chariot, it will be a great deception." It seems that this Author wanted to hold a position midway between the skepticism of the unbelievers and the crude imaginings of the people. He desires that one recognize and honor spirits, but that one not believe them existing in such a manner as the imagination may represent it.

§53   The same Chinese philosopher [Zhu Xi], page 39, discussing the Spirit of Heaven, which is the King-on-high, says that it is called Xin, because the air of Heaven extends everywhere. Father Longobardi infers from this (12:64) that the Chinese believe that there is no living and intelligent spirit in heaven, only the substance of air, with its activity or influence. But the good Father sees here only his own prejudices. The Chinese author attributes to spirits not only force or activity, but intelligence as well, since they evoke fear and respect. He considers the air itself, that is its subtle bodies, only as their vehicle.

§54   [Zhu Xi] also seeks a relationship or sense of proportion between the Spirit to whom one sacrifices and he who sacrifices. That is why the Emperor must sacrifice to the King-on-high or the Lord of Heaven, and thus he is called Tien Zu[141] son of Heaven. Princes and Dukes sacrifice to

---

[140] See fn. 112.

[141] *Tian zi* 天 子 , "Son of Heaven."

the protecting Spirits of the five ways of life. Scholars sacrifice to Confucius in the schools of the Universities. This relationship also requires further that each person sacrifice to his ancestors. From this, [Zhu Xi] wants to indicate that the Spirits govern according to order and aid those who conform to it. Whereas Father Longobardi concludes from these passages (12:65) that Spirits are made up only of air and matter, the Chinese Author actually suggests the opposite.

§54a   I have also found another rather charming line of reasoning against idolators in this Chinese Philosophy. The scholar Ching-Lu[142] explains the Chung-Jung of Confucius (Book 28, page 37)—as reported by Father Longobardi himself (12:60)—saying that it is quite stupid to ask for rain from wooden and earthen idols, which are inside Temples, while neglecting the mountains and the waters, that is, those things whose vapors produce the rain. He suggests that reverence should be grounded on reason, by observing the relations and proportions between things; only then is it acceptable to the spirits, or rather to the Xangti, to the Universal Spirit, or if you wish, to the Li, to the supreme reason which governs all. Now the good Father penetrates very little into [the author's] meaning when he concludes from this that the latter recognizes the existence of no other Spirit in the waters and mountains than that of corporeal air, which is without consciousness.

§54b   In the same vein, Confucius says in his Su Lum Iu[143] (by the account of Father de S.-Marie, p. 29): that to sacrifice to a spirit not of your station and situation or not fitting for you is foolhardy and futile flattery; justice and reason find it repugnant. Now according to the account of Chum Ko Lao,[144] it is the province only of the Emperor to sacrifice to Heaven and Earth; only the Heroes of the Kingdom sacrifice to the mountains and the waters; and only illustrious men sacrifice to the Spirits; the rest of the people are responsible for the sacrifices to their ancestors.

---

[142] Cheng Yi. See the Introduction, p. 27, and note 78. The reference is not to the *Zhong Yong,* but to Cheng Yi's commentary thereon in the *Compendium,* from which Longobardi is translating.

[143] Must be a reference to the *Lun Yu,* 2:24.

[144] This term appears twice in the *Mission Treatise:* once as CHVM KO LAO, and once as CHAM KO LAO. In neither place is a context provided that suggests a reference for the term. One possible expression for Ko Lao, however, is "Grand Secretary" (see *Preface,* fn. 6), and consequently the name may refer to a high official of Ming–Qing times who wrote on ritual observances, perhaps Zhang Juzheng 張 居 正 (1525–1582). See Lundbaek, p. 37.

The Philosophical Summa [Xing Li] says (in F. de S.-Marie, p. 31) that souls seek Spirits of the same quality and those with which they have the best rapport. For example, if a peasant addressed himself to the spirit of a man of station, he would be immediately rebuffed and the spirit would do nothing. But if someone invokes a spirit appropriate to his station, he is assured that he will affect the spirit and cause it to favor him. Now the F. de S.-Marie adds (p. 32) that only scholars sacrifice to Confucius and that it is in this way that one should understand what Father Martinius divulged in Rome in 1656, namely that the temple, or as it is called, the Hall of Confucius, is closed to everyone but scholars. The same Father notes (p. 50) that Chinese soldiers revere an ancient and illustrious captain, Tai-Kung, doctors a Chinese Asclepius, goldsmiths an ancient Alchemist, whom they call Su-Hoang.[145]

§55 This father goes into further detail (p. 95). According to him, the Chinese ascribe to the very exalted Xangti, and to all the other Spirits, Kwei-Xin, the governance of the world. The former governs as a sovereign Lord who inhabits Heaven as his palace, and the latter govern as his ministers, each overseeing the position which has been entrusted to him: the Sun, moon, stars, clouds, thunder, hail, storms and rain; earth, mountains, lakes, rivers, crops, fruits, forests, and the grass; humans and animals, houses, doorways, wells, kitchens, furnaces and even the most unclean places; and still others oversee war, the sciences, medicine, agriculture, navigation and all the technical arts. Each Chinese takes for his Patron a spirit to whom he prays, whom he invokes, and to whom he sacrifices in order to be treated favorably. Each also renders to his ancestors the same obligations rendered to familiar and domestic spirits; [nonfamilial] dead are treated as strangers. They pray to Confucius and his

---

[145] Ste.-Marie provides no more information about these figures than Leibniz gives here, making the task of identifying them difficult, because the Chinese pantheon of minor deities and patron saints is very large. "Tai-Kung" is probably the military hero of the Three Kingdoms period Guan Yu 關 羽 , better known as Guan Di 關 帝 , or Guan Gong 關 公 . He was one of the most popular of all heroes in China. There are many patron saints and gods having to do with medicine, but the "Chinese Asclepius" is probably Yao Wang 藥 王 (ca. ninth century BCE), whose given name was Sun Simiao 孫 思 邈 . "Su Hoang" is probably a reference to the second century BCE magician Dongfang So 東 方 朔 , legendarily an incarnation of the planet Venus, and the protector of those who work with metals. See also Werner.

most renowned disciples as the Spirits who preside over the Schools and the sciences. The Father adds that the Chinese are like the Stoics, who pictured a material God suffused throughout the Universe in order to move it, and to govern it with other, subaltern gods. But I find nothing which prevents us from finding here a spiritual God, author of matter itself, displaying His wisdom and power in brute things and served by intelligent spirits similar to our own angels and souls. And one could thus say that the average Chinese, like the pagans, multiply individual spirits beyond measure and need, while wise men content themselves with a belief in the Supreme spirit and in his ministers in general, without assigning them fixed ministries.

§56   I said at the outset that I did not want to examine to what extent the manner of worship of the Chinese could be condemned or justified, and that I only wanted to investigate their doctrines [end of §1]. It seems to me (to bring everything together) that the intent of their sages was to venerate the Li or supreme reason—which made itself visible and operative everywhere—be it directly in brute objects where intelligence is appropriate only to their author, or be it through lower spirits, serving as ministers (with whom virtuous souls are associated). The very same sages wanted attention given to objects in which the Supreme wisdom appears more particularly, and that each one render homage in the prescribed ways to the objects appropriate to his station. The Emperor will render homage, and defer, to Heaven and Earth; the great Lords to the great bodies which have an influence in the production of food (such as the elements, the rivers, the mountains); the scholars to the spirits of great philosophers and legislators; and everyone to the virtuous souls of their families. Father de S.-Marie (p. 25) records an outstanding passage, where the Chinese interpreters tell us that two characters—Ty Chang[146]—are uttered to honor one's ancestors. Here is their explanation: when the Emperor sacrifices to his ancestors, he must elevate his spirit and reflect upon the

---

[146] Although Ste.-Marie does not cite a source, he is probably making reference to the *Li Ji* chapter (Legge, vol. I, pp. 223–25) in which the sacrifices of the Emperor and nobles are specified. Four of the major sacrifices related to the seasons, and those for summer and autumn were named *di* 禘 and *chang* 嘗, which were later used together as names of the highest ancestral sacrifices. At times *di* was used this way alone, as in *Lun Yu* 3:10 and 3:11. In neither of these classical texts, however, is it mentioned that the names of these sacrifices were to be uttered while performing them.

creator from which his first ancestor is descended, and address his sacrifice to both of these combined. (But not as if they were equals; this is, I believe, how one should understand it.) Father S.-Marie here adds that the ancient interpretation of these characters says the same thing; that the letter Ti signifies that, in sacrificing to their ancestors, worshippers relate through their sacrifices to the origins from whence they came and to which they will return at death; always careful, however, of the order of precedence of ancestors. In other words, the souls of the ancestors are regarded as subaltern spirits to the supreme spirit and universal Lord of Heaven and Earth.

[III. *Chinese Opinion Concerning the Human Soul, its Immortality, Rewards and Punishments*]

§57 We have spoken of the First Principle, author and governor of things, known under the name of the Li, Taikie or Xangti, according to the Chinese, and then of his ministers, the subaltern spirits called Xin, Tunxin,[147] Kuei-Xin. To complete their theology, one has to speak of human souls, which—when they are separated from gross bodies—are called Hoën by F. Longobardi (8:44), and more often Ling-Hoën[148]

---

[147] This is the first (and only) mention of "Tunxin" in the *Discourse*. The term does not occur in either Longobardi or Ste.-Marie, and there is no close analogue for it in this context. The two most likely candidates are: (1) *Tu-shen* 土 神, "spirits of the earth," which Ste. Marie writes as "Tv Xin" (pp. 77 and 122); or (2) *qun-shen* 群 神, the "hosts of spirits." This latter term occurs in the *Shu Jing* chapter discussed by Leibniz in §45. The *Pian* sacrifice (fn. 128) was offered to the *Qun shen*.

[148] *Hun* 魂 and *ling-hun* 靈 魂. The *hun* is the spiritual element of human souls, as opposed to the *bo* 魄, or material element. The *bo* did not leave the body at death, and if the deceased were properly buried and sacrificed to thereafter, the material soul would remain at peace in the grave with the body, while the *hun* became a *shen* 神, spirit, and aided descendants. If the body was not properly cared for, however, the *bo* left it and became a *gui* (ghost); and caused mischief. *Ling-hun* is another name for the spiritual soul, but more specifically connotes the active power, efficacy, and sphere of influence which the spiritual soul had with respect to the descendants of the departed. When the sacrifices to the ancestors have been minimally neglected—not neglected enough for the material soul to become a *gui*—their spiritual souls would wander about, and in this state would be called *you-hun* 幽 魂 (see below, fn. 154). For additional materials dealing with the Chinese concept of the soul, especially translations, see De Groot, vols. I and III.

(Preface, p. 6 and 2:19). Sing-Hoën are mentioned by Father de S.-Marie (p. 58), but I suspect a printer's error, although I am not positively certain of this because the same Father says further on (p. 93) that deceased men are called Sin-Kuei,[149] which he says means retired from mortal life. It is true that for the Chinese, souls are subsumed in some fashion under spirits, and are integral to their worship; souls merit, however, a separate discussion, in order to know what Chinese scholars teach concerning the nature of these Spirits and their state after this life.

§58   Father Longobardi asserts (1:14) that the earliest Chinese texts, speaking of the human soul under the name of Ling-Hoën, lead us to understand that it endures after the death of the body. This is why it is said in the Xi-King,[150] Book 6, page 1, that Vuen Vuang, ancient king of China, is on high in Heaven; he is at the side of the Xangti or the King-on-high, Lord of Heaven, and that he is at times rising, at times descending (2:14–15:83). The separated soul is also called Jeu-Hoën,[151] wandering soul (ibid., p. 83), which means freely, I believe, animula vagula blandula.[152] Doctor Paul,[153] a Christian scholar, doubts, however (according to Father Longobardi), whether the Chinese have any knowledge of the true God, but nevertheless believe that regarding the soul, they did have some knowledge of it, though quite confused (17:100). This allows enough of an opening for knowledgeable missionaries to enlighten them and to clear up their confusion. Let us begin this task.

§59   The Chinese say (Longobardi, 15:81) that the death of man is only the separation of the elements of which it is composed, and which return after this separation to the places which are proper to them. Thus the Hoën, or soul, rises to Heaven; the Pe[154] or the body, returns to the earth. This is what is said in the Xu-King, Book I, p. 16, where the death of

---

[149] *Shen gui* 神 鬼 , reversing the order.

[150] *Shi Jing.* See Legge, vol. IV, pp. 428–29. "Vuen Vuang" is King Wen (fn. 97).

[151] See fn. 148.

[152] I.e., "wandering soul."

[153] Xu Guangqi 徐 光 啓 (1562–1633), Ricci's most famous convert to Christianity. He wrote, and translated with Ricci, works on astronomy, mathematics, and agriculture. His descendants remained one of China's most influential Christian families through the present century.

[154] While Leibniz refers to the physical *body* here, the term *Pe* is almost surely *bo* 魄 . See fn. 148.

King Iao[155] is described in these terms: "he has risen and descended." The commentary explains it in this manner; "he has risen and descended" means he is dead, because when a man dies, his essence of fire and air (the commentator means the animated air, the Soul) rises to Heaven, and the body returns to earth. This author speaks almost as if he had read the Holy Scriptures. So, too does the Author of the Chinese Philosophy who speaks of this matter in Book 28, about page 41, where he records this sentence of Chin-Zu:[156] when the composition of man occurs and he comes into this world—that is, when Heaven and Earth are united—Universal Nature does not come (for it is already present). When man dies—that is when Heaven and Earth are separated—Universal Nature does not leave (for it is always everywhere). But the air, which is of the essence of Heaven, returns to Heaven; and the corporeal element, which is of the essence of the earth, returns to earth.

§60 It also appears that some Chinese scholars regard men, and especially great men, as angels incarnate. A certain Chinese Doctor Michael,[157] a Christian, but one partial to Chinese doctrines, said in his preface to the explanation of the Ten Commandments that the ancient savants of China had been Spirits or incarnated Angels, one succeeding the other. And with respect to the greatest men, he goes so far as to claim that the Xangti itself or the supreme Spirit has been incarnated in them, as for example in the personages of Iao, of Xun, of Confucius and of others. This is doubtless an error, for such an incarnation is fitting only to Jesus Christ, and his words show well that this doctor is only quasi-Christian. But he did not believe, however, that he would do violence to long-standing Chinese doctrine in denying that the soul is a fleeting and evanescent thing, [by saying that] an incarnate angel subsists before birth and after death. This doctrine is in accord with that of Plato and Origen.[158] Another Chinese

---

[155] Emperor Yao (see fn. 124). The reference to the *Shu Jing* does mention Yao's death, but not his "rising and descending," which was Zhu Xi's commentary on this passage. See Legge, vol. III, pp. 40–41.

[156] In this section of the *Compendium*, Cheng Yi (see fn. 142) is the author, who must therefore be the "Chin-zu" referred to here.

[157] Yang Ting-yun 楊 廷 筠 (1557–1627), another influential convert of Ricci's.

[158] Plato's belief in the pre-existence of the soul, based on the argument from recollection (ANAMNESIS) is first presented in the *Meno* (81; 85D–86B) and further developed in the *Phaedo*

doctor, friend of the Christians, testified to Father Longobardi that he had opinions on this matter quite close to Father Michael.

§61 Father de S.-Marie reports (p. 76) that the Chinese believe that Confucius and the sage kings and the ancient philosophers of their land—who were oracles by excellence of their virtue—were all incarnations of God in Heaven, Xangti in the Kingdom of China. The Father supports this by citing the views of some ancient philosophers, and of the Manicheans according to Augustine, and by the views of the Averroists and of Spinoza, who made the soul a part or modification of God, which does not have a separate existence after death. But on this account, great men would have nothing over others in this respect, and since the souls of those who are angels incarnate subsist after death, why wouldn't the soul of one who is incomparably greater subsist, if God supreme is united to this Soul and to its body in a particular fashion?

§62 Thus I see nothing which prevents us from, and much that is favorable to, our claiming rather that human souls, according to the classical doctrine of the Chinese, resemble the nature of Spirits, ministers of the Supreme Spirit—although they are to a degree inferior to them. I am not at all surprised that Father Longobardi and Father de S.-Marie are opposed to this opinion, since heterodox and atheistic scholars (who are permitted in China to utter their impieties with impunity, at least orally) presented them with strange views, current in China today, but which are directly contrary to ancient doctrine and to religious practices instituted over 3,000 years ago in the Chinese Empire. These [contemporary] views claim: (1) that the Li itself (supreme Reason), or the supreme Spirits (Xangti, as the substance of this Order or Reason) and all the intelligent Spirits which serve him are only fictions; (2) that the supreme Spirit or

---

(72E–77A). Though there are scattered references throughout Plato to the soul's immortality, or rather eternality (e.g., *Meno* 86B; *Phaedrus* 245C–246A), the main arguments are found in the *Phaedo* and form the bulk of this dialogue. Many Church Fathers, such as Sts. Basil and Gregory, believed that angels and other spirits were created before the material universe. Origen in particular "was led by his strongly Platonist leanings to affirm [the soul's] pre-existence and explained its confinement in a body as a punishment for sins committed in its previous incorporeal state." Article on "Soul," *The Oxford Dictionary of the Christian Church*, p. 1273. See Origen, *De Principiis*, I, vi, 2; I, viii; I, ix. On the immortality and ethereality of the soul, see *ibid.*, IV, i, 36; II, iv, 7. See also §2, above.

universal principle is nothing other than prime matter or corporeal air and nothing more; (3) that the Spirits offered to the common people for veneration are portions of this air; and (4) that all occurs by accident or by necessity in a brutish fashion, without any wisdom, providence or justice directing it; so that talk of Chinese religion is only a farce. But as this imputation is ill-founded in every way, both with regard to God and to the Angels, as we have amply demonstrated, one may judge as well that the same obtains with respect to souls.

§63   I find nothing that these Fathers bring forth from the passages of the classical authors, early or later, which sufficiently favors their allegations concerning the human soul, any more than their allegations concerning God and the angels. These Fathers give only interpretations grafted on from without, which strain or even destroy the texts and render them ridiculous, contradictory and deceitful. Father Longobardi, given what we have reported of his views—namely, that according to the Chinese, death separates the terrestrial from the celestial, which is aerial and firelike in nature and returns to Heaven—concludes from this that souls are something purely material which are dissolved in the air or in the ether. But by the same reasoning, one could say that Angels are nothing but fire, since God, according to Holy Scriptures, fecit Ministros suos flammam ignis.[159] One should rather say that these Spirits are spiritual substances, though they are clothed in subtle material bodies. So has antiquity, both pagan and Christian, ordinary conceived of the genii, Angels and Demons. The soul returns to Heaven, and is more united than before to the celestial matter diffused everywhere, and thus more capable of conforming to the will of God, quite like the angels it resembles.[160] So have the ancient Chinese apparently understood it, when they have said that the soul is joined again to Heaven, and to the Xangti.

§64   These Fathers, or rather those who have given their impressions to the Fathers, having misused the Chinese axiom that everything is one—i.e., that all participates in the one—would have us believe that according to the Chinese everything is only matter but in different dispositions; that the Xangti itself is only that [i.e., matter], and so too is the Li—"Reason" or primitive substance—and that everything participates in

---

[159] "He made a flame of fire to be His servants." A paraphrase of the Vulgate, Psalm 103, 4.

[160] See §2 and fn. 7.

matter's perfection according to its own measure of the same. Consequently, they would want the return of the soul to be nothing other than its dissolution into ethereal matter, it losing all knowledge gained through its bodily organs. They could say, with even more likelihood, conforming to the opinions of the Manicheans and the Averroists, that God or the Li or the Xangti is the soul of the world, which creates individual souls by acting on organic bodies, and which puts an end to them as soon as they are decomposed. But besides the fact that these opinions are also contrary to reason and to the nature of the individual,[161] these opinions are also contrary to the passage from the Chinese Author (cited by Father Longobardi) who clearly distinguishes the Universal Nature—the Li and the Xangti—from the particular nature of the soul. The Universal Nature (the Chinese author says), neither comes nor goes, but the soul comes and goes, rises and descends. That is, it is sometimes united to a coarse body, sometimes to a more subtle and noble one, and this gives us to understand that it continues to subsist, for otherwise it would return to the Universal Nature.

§64a   Now let us see how Father de S.-Marie speaks about it (p. 40): the Chinese have various errors concerning human souls. Some believe that they do not die at all, that they simply move on and proceed to animate different bodies, human and animal, where they are reborn. Others believe that they descend into Hell from whence they come out after some time.[162] Still other Chinese acknowledge the souls as immortal, claiming that they wander in the farthest mountains, calling these souls Xin-Sien,[163] under which name they have certain chapels dedicated to them. The literati and the better educated believe that our souls are small portions of subtle air or a firelike and celestial vapor, detached from the most subtle matter of Heaven from whence they draw their origins; which, once they leave their bodies, rise again to Heaven which is their center and from whence they issue and where again they intermingle. The Chinese Philosophical Summa Singlitaciven,[164] Vol. 28—a treatise concerning the soul and the

---

[161] See §23.

[162] Buddhists held the first view, and some Buddhists and many Daoists held the second.

[163] *Shen xian* 神 仙 , another name for "Immortals." (See fn. 108). This was a fairly pervasive view in China.

[164] The *Compendium.* Leibniz is quoting Ste.-Marie directly.

body—says that the suitable and true origin of the ethereal soul is in Heaven, to which the ethereal soul soars [after death] to become one and the same substance with it. The origin of the body is the Earth into which it dissolves and transforms itself [after death]. The author of this particular work is from a later time and his authority does not approach that of the ancients. However, one need not ignore this passage. I believe that the translation of it suffers somewhat from the prejudice of the translator [i.e., St.-Marie], when he states that the soul becomes the same substance with Heaven. Perhaps the Chinese author only wants to say that the two are united after death. But even if the passage were to say what [St.-Marie] makes it say, such very general expressions can always be given a positive meaning. For all celestial spirits are of the substance of Heaven, and the soul, becoming a celestial Spirit, becomes thereby of the same substance with Heaven. But by Heaven is understood the whole celestial Hierarchy, exercitus Coelorum,[165] under the Grand Monarch of the Universe. This Heaven is not simply the visible sky, for according to the opinions of the Chinese cited above, Heaven's air (with its celestial Spirits) extends everywhere. Thus it is not necessary, according to them, to conceive of souls as completely distinct from Heaven. To talk of wandering here and there in the mountains, rising and descending, being at the side of the Xangti, and so forth, are only imagistic ways of speaking.

§65 The [Chinese concept] of immortality of the soul will become clearer if one interprets ancient Chinese doctrine as saying that souls receive reward and punishment after this life. It is true that the Literati sect [i.e., the Confucians] speak neither of Paradise nor Hell, and the Chinese Christian, Dr. Michael, regretfully acknowledges this (17:95) in praising the sect of Foë which propounds both.[166] It also appears that modern Chinese, who wish to pass for being the most enlightened, ridicule this [Buddhist] view when one talks to them of another life (17:89). But perhaps they will not always ridicule it if they consider that this supreme substance —which on their own grounds is the source of wisdom and justice—could not act less perfectly on the spirits and the souls which it creates, than a wise king in his realm acts upon his subjects whom he did not create of his own will, and whom it is more difficult for him to govern since they do not

---

[165] "The Army of the Heavens."

[166] Ironically, the view which Leibniz applauds here and in the next paragraph comes from Buddhism, not Confucianism.

depend upon him absolutely. Thus this Kingdom of the Spirits under this great Master cannot be less orderly than a Kingdom of men, and consequently it follows that virtue should be rewarded and vice punished under this governance, justice being insufficiently done in this life.

§65a   This is also what the ancient Chinese have suggested. We have already noted that they place a wise and virtuous Emperor at the side of the Xangti and that they consider the souls of great men as angels incarnate. Father de S.-Marie (p. 27) cites the Xi-King (one of the five principal books of the literati), which makes mention of some of their ancient kings, who after their death, rise to Heaven in order to enlighten and help (I believe this should be translated "to assist and serve") this very exalted king <u>Xanti</u>, and to sit at his right and left side.[167] It is said in the same book that these kings, rising from the earth to Heaven, and descending from Heaven to earth, can favor and abet the Kingdom as its patrons and protectors.[168]

§66   The worship of ancestors and great men instituted by the ancient Chinese can indeed have for its goals: to display the gratitude of the living as they cherish the rewards of Heaven, and to excite men to perform actions which render them worthy of the recognition of posterity. However, the ancients speak as if the Spirits of virtuous ancestors, surrounded by the aura of glory at the Court of the Monarch of the Universe, were capable of obtaining good and evil for their descendants. And it appears by this at least that they have conceived of them as continuing to subsist.

§66a   It is instructive to see how they explicate this matter. According to the account of Father de S.-Marie (p. 21ff.), Confucius makes the Emperor Xum[169] author of the Ancestor worship (Chung-Jung, Chpt. 17); this Emperor was the fifth after the Foundation of the Monarch (according to the Tung-Kien)[170]—i.e., the Royal Chronology, or Universal History, one of the classical texts). Confucius praises him in the extreme and

---

[167] This is Ste.-Marie's interpretation of the same *Shi Jing* passage cited by Leibniz *via* Longobardi in §58. The "author" referred to below is Zhu Xi.

[168] Leibniz is quoting Ste.-Marie directly, except for the parenthetical remark.

[169] Shun. See fn. 124.

[170] *Zi-zhi tong jian* 資 治 通 鑑 , known as the *Comprehensive Mirror,* is a major history of China written by the famous scholar and statesman, Sima Guang 司 馬 光 , (1018–1086). It is not clear from Longobardi's text that he has used this work, however. More probably he was using the *Tong-jian gang mu* 通 鑑 綱 目 —*Outline of the Comprehensive Mirror*—an abridgment of Sima Guang's work by Zhu Xi.

attributes the prosperity of the Empire to the worship he instituted and also Ch. 78,[171] in which he proffers the ancient kings as models for posterity. He also says towards the end of this chapter that anyone who understood perfectly what the worship of Heaven and Earth comprised, and the proper reason for sacrificing to his ancestors, would be able to assure himself a peaceful prosperity and a wise government throughout the kingdom with as much certainty as if he held them in his very hand.[172]

§67   It is true that the Chinese scholars speak neither of Hell nor of purgatory, but it is possible that some among them believe or have believed at other times that the wandering souls which prowl here and there in the mountains and the forests are in a sort of purgatory. We have already spoken of these wandering souls.[173] Without making too much of a comparison between the opinions of the Christians and the pagans, one could nevertheless say that there is something approaching this in the life of St. Conrad, a Bishop of Constance, whose biography is published in the second volume of my collection,[174] where it is recorded that he and his friend St. Udalric discovered souls in the form of birds condemned to the waterfalls of the Rhine which they saved by their prayers. So too, perhaps, according to some of these Chinese literati, ancient or modern, souls deserving of punishment become spirits destined to lowly stations, guarding doors and tending kitchens and furnaces until they have expiated themselves. We are not sufficiently conversant with the doctrine of the scholars on these matters to go into detail about them.

[IV. *Concerning the Characters which Fohi, Founder of the Chinese Empire, Used in His Writings, and Binary Arithmetic*]

§68   It is indeed apparent that if we Europeans were well enough informed concerning Chinese Literature, then, with the aid of logic, critical thinking, mathematics and our manner of expressing thought—

---

[171] Ste.-Marie and Leibniz have 78 here, but it should be 19.

[172] This well-known example can also be found in *Lun Yu* 3:11, and in the *Li Ji* (Legge, vol II, p. 272).

[173] In §58 and §64a.

[174] *Scriptores Rerum Brunsvicensium*. Hanover: N. Foerster, v. II (1710), 7–8.

more exacting than theirs—we could uncover in the Chinese writings of the remotest antiquity many things unknown to modern Chinese and even to other commentators thought to be classical. Reverend Father Bouvet and I have discovered the meaning, apparently truest to the text, of the characters of Fohi, founder of Empire, which consist simply of combinations of unbroken and broken lines, and which pass for the most ancient writing of China in its simplest form. There are 64 figures contained in the book called Ye Kim,[175] that is, the Book of Changes. Several centuries after Fohi, the Emperor Ven Vam[176] and his son Cheu Cum, and Confucius more than five centuries later, have all sought therein philosophical mysteries. Others have even wanted to extract from them a sort of Geomancy and other follies. Actually, the 64 figures represent a Binary Arithmetic which apparently this great legislator [Fu Xi] possessed, and which I have rediscovered some thousands of years later.

§68a   In Binary Arithmetic, there are only two signs, 0 and 1, with which one can write all numbers.[177] When I communicated this system to the Reverend Father Bouvet, he recognized in it the characters of Fohi, for the numbers 0 and 1 correspond to them exactly[178] if we put a broken line for 0 and unbroken line for the unity, 1. This Arithmetic furnishes the simplest way of making changes, since there are only two components, concerning which I wrote a small essay in my early youth, which was reprinted a long time afterwards against my will.[179] So it seems that Fohi had insight into the science of combinations, but the Arithmetic having been completely lost, later Chinese have not taken care to think of them in

---

[175] *Yi Jing.* See Introduction, pp. 20–22.

[176] Again, King Wen; this time the spelling is Bouvet's. "Cheu Cum" is Zhou Gong 周 公 , the Duke of Zhou, and King Wu's brother. He was one of Confucius's favorite culture heroes.

[177] At this point Leibniz wrote, but then crossed out, the following: "I have since found that it further expresses the logic of dichotomies which is of the greatest use, if one always retains an exact opposition between the numbers of the division."

[178] At this point, Leibniz wrote, but then crossed out the following: "provided that one places before a number as many zeroes as necessary so that the least of the numbers has as many lines as the greatest."

[179] In a letter to Rémond in July 1714, Leibniz wrote about "a little schoolboyish essay called 'On the Art of Combinations,' published in 1666, and later reprinted without my permission." Gerhardt, III, 620. See Loemker, p. 657.

this [arithmetical] way and they have made of these characters of Fohi some kind of symbols and Hieroglyphs, as one customarily does when one has strayed from the true meaning (as the good Father Kirker[180] has done with respect to the script of the Egyptian obelisks of which he understands nothing). Now this shows also that the ancient Chinese have surpassed the modern ones in the extreme, not only in piety (which is the basis of the most perfect morality) but in science as well.

§69   Since this Binary Arithmetic, although explained in the Miscellany of Berlin,[181] is still little known, and the mention of its parallelism with the characters of Fohi is found only in the German journal of the year 1705 of the late Mr. Tenzelius,[182] I want to explain it here—where it appears to be very appropriate—since it concerns justification of the doctrines of the ancient Chinese and their superiority over the moderns. I will only add before turning to this matter that the late Mr. Andreas Müller, native of Greiffenhagen, Provost of Berlin, a man of Europe, who without ever having left it, had studied the Chinese characters closely, and published with notes, what Abdalla Beidavaeus wrote on China. This Arab author remarks that Fohi had found a peculiare scribendi genus, Arithmeticam, contratus et Rationaria, "a peculiar manner of writing, of arithmetic, of contracts, and of accounts."[183] What he says confirms my explanation of the characters of this ancient philosopher-king whereby they are reduced to numbers.

§70   The ancient Romans made use of a mixed arithmetic, quinary

---

[180] Athanasius Kircher. See Introduction, p. 11 and n. 27.

[181] "De periodis columnarum in serie numerorum progressionis Arithmeticae Dyadice expressorum," by P. Dangicourt, in *Miscellanea Berolinensia,* I (1701), 336–376. This and the Tenzel article cited below were both instigated by Leibniz himself. See Zacher, p. 1.

[182] "Erklärung der Arithmeticae binariae, . . .," in *Curieuse bibliothic oder Fortsetzung der Monatlichen Unterredungen einiger guten Freunde,* ed. W.E. Tenzel (Frankfurt and Leipzig, 1705), pp. 81–112. See Zacher, p. 210. Leibniz omits mention of his own, earlier endeavor concerning binary arithmetic and its relationship to the characters of Fu Xi, written in 1703; "Explication de l'Arithmetique Binaire qui se sert des seuls caracters 0 et 1; avec des Remarques sur son utilité, et sur ce qu'elle donne le sens des anciennes figures Chinoises de Fohi," par M. Leibniz, *Histoire de l'Academie royale des Sciences, Année 1703;* avec les Memoires . . . pour la meme Année, Paris 1705 [Mem.], pp. 85–89. A more readable and available edition of this work is found in Zacher, pp. 293–301.

[183] There is little evidence that the hexagrams were used for these purposes. Leibniz is quoting directly from Tenzel. See also Zacher, p. 159. And see *Remarks,* §9.

and denary, and one still sees reminders of it in their counters.[184] One sees, from Archimedes' work on the counting of the sand,[185] that already in his time something approaching denary arithmetic was understood (which has come down to us from the Arabs and which appears to have been brought from Spain, or at least made more known by the renowned Gerbert, later Pope, under the name of Sylvester II[186]). This prevalence of base 10 arithmetic seems to come from the fact that we have 10 fingers, but as this number is arbitrary, some have proposed counting by dozens, and dozens of dozens, etc.[187] On the other hand, the late Mr. Erhard Weigelius resorts to a lesser number predicated on the quaternary or Tetractys like the Pythagoreans;[188] thus, just as in the decimal progression we write all numbers using 0, 1, 2, 3, 4, 5, 6, 7, 8, 9, he would write all numbers in his quaternary progression using 0, 1, 2, 3; for example 321 for him signifies $3 \times 4^2 + 2 \times 4^1 + 1$ or rather $48 + 16 + 1$, that is 65 according to the ordinary system.

---

[184] Leibniz is talking of the Roman numerals, which except for unity (I), are based on either five (V, L, D) or ten (X, C, M), hence the mixed nature of their numeration or counting, but not necessarily of their arithmetic, about which little is known. The purpose of the Roman counters, originally pebbles (*calculi*), is uncertain; it has been argued that they were used in games such as backgammon or checkers, or even like poker chips. See Smith, II, 165–66.

[185] "Archimedes saw the defects of the Greek number system, and in his *Sand Reckoner* he suggested an elaborate scheme of numeration, arranging the numbers in octads, or the eighth powers of ten." *Ibid.*, I, 113.

[186] Gerbert, who was pope from 999 to 1003, has traditionally been held responsible for introducing the Arabic numerals into Christian Europe, which he probably learned while studying in Spain. Leibniz is wrong in thinking that Gerbert introduced the decimal or denary system, rather than simply the nine characters. "He probably did not know of the zero, and at any rate he did not know its real significance." *Ibid.*, II, 74–75; see also, *Ibid.*, I, 195–196.

[187] Leibniz himself toyed briefly with a base 12 (and even mentioned a base 16) number system and may have gotten the idea from Pascal. See Zacher, pp. 17–21.

[188] Erhard Weigel (1625–1699) was professor of Mathematics at the University of Jena, where Leibniz followed his lectures for one semester in 1663. Having been influenced strongly by the Pythagorean and other mystical traditions in mathematics, Weigel saw the number 4 as the perfect number and constructed a base 4 number system. Although Weigel influenced Leibniz in many areas (e.g., the need for linguistic and legal reforms in Germany), the latter saw no need for such a number system. Practically, a base 10 or even higher number system (12 or 16) shortened calculations and condensed enumeration; theoretically, a base 2 system was best, since it had the simplest and most easily analyzable base. Couturat, pp. 473–474.

§71 This gives me the opportunity to point out that all numbers could be written by 0 and 1 in the binary or dual progression. Thus:

1	1	10 is equal to 2
10	2	100 is equal to 4
1000	8	1000 is equal to 8
10000	16	etc.
100000	32	
1000000	64	

And accordingly, numbers are expressed as follows:

0	0
1	1
10	2
11	3
100	4
101	5
110	6
111	7
1000	8
1001	9
1010	10
1011	11
1100	12
1101	13
1110	14
1111	15
10000	16
10001	17
10010	18
10011	19
10100	20
10101	21
10110	22
10111	23
11000	24
11001	25
11010	26
11011	27
11100	28
11101	29
11110	30
11111	31
100000	32
etc.	etc.

These terms correspond with the hypothesis; for example:

$$111 = 100 + 10 + 1 = 4 + 2 + 1 = 7$$
$$11001 = 10000 + 1000 + 1 = 16 + 4 + 1 = 25 \text{[189]}$$

They can also be found by continual addition of unity, for example:

```
    1
   .1
   10
    1
   11
   .1
  100
    1
  101
   .1
  110
    1
  111
   .1
 1000
```

The points denote unity which is kept in mind in ordinary calculation.[190]

---

[189] The mistake is Leibniz's; *4* should be *8*. This section should be read together with *Remarks* §9.

[190] See §72 for explanation.

§71a   But, to continue, if one wishes to make a table expressing terms for all the natural numbers in order, one need not calculate, since it is sufficient to note that each column is periodic, the same periodicity recurring ad infinitum: the first column runs 0, 1, 0, 1, 0, 1, etc.; the second 0, 0, 1, 1, 0, 0, 1, 1, etc.; the third 0, 0, 0, 0, 1, 1, 1, 1, 0, 0, 0, 0, 1, 1, 1, 1, etc.; the fourth 0, 0, 0, 0, 0, 0, 0, 0, 1, 1, 1, 1, 1, 1, 1, 1, 0, 0, 0, 0, 0, 0, 0, 0, 1, 1, 1, 1, 1, 1, 1, 1, etc. And so on with further columns, assuming that the empty places above each column are filled with zeroes. Thus one can write these columns at once and accordingly make up the table of natural numbers without any calculations. This is what one can call enumeration.

§72   As for addition, it is simply done by counting and making periods when there are numbers to add together, adding up each column as usual, which will be done as follows: count the unities of the column; for example, for 29, look how this number is written in the table, to wit, by 11101; thus you write 1 under the column and put periods under the second, third and fourth column thereafter. These periods denote that it is necessary to count out one unity further in the column following.

§73   Subtraction is just as easy. Multiplication is reduced to simple additions and has no need of the Pythagorean table, it sufficing to know that 0 times 0 is 0, that 0 times 1 is 0, that 1 times 0 is 0, and that 1 times 1 is 1.

§74   In division there is no need to tally as in ordinary calculation. One must only see if the divisor is greater or less than the preceding remainder.

§75   These are simplifications that have been proposed by a clever man since the introduction of this Arithmetic into certain calculations.[191] But the principal utility of this binary system is that it can do much to perfect the science of numbers because all calculations are made according to periodicity. It is some achievement that the numerical powers of the

---

[191] Leibniz is referring to *Arithmeticus perfectus, Qui Tria numerare nescit, seu Arithmetic dualis* (Prague, 1712) by W. J. Pelican. Pelican apparently showed how one can use the binary system for other calculations as well, i.e., fractional arithmetic, roots, and proportions. See Zacher, p. 211.

same order, made by raising the ordered natural numbers, however high the order, never have a greater number of periods than the natural numbers themselves which are their roots. . . . [Text breaks off at this point.]

Transcription Conversion Table

Pinyin	Wade-Giles
b	p
c	ts', tz'
ch	ch'
d	t
g	k
ian	ien
j	ch
k	k'
ong	ung
p	p'
q	ch'
r	j
si	szu
t	t'
x	hs
yu	u
you	yu
yu	yü
z	ts,tz
zh	ch
-i (zhi)	-ih (chih)
zi	tzu

Selected Bibliography

Note: Standard philosophical works, *except* for those of Leibniz, are cited in the notes, but not listed below unless a quotation was taken from a particular edition. While this bibliography is by no means complete, it is intended to be fairly comprehensive of the materials covered in the text.

Works of Leibniz

Viri illustris Godefridi Guil. Leibnitii epistolae ad diversos. . . . Ed. Kortholt, C., 4 vols. Leipzig: B.C. Breitkopf, 1734–1742.

G.G. Leibnitii: Opera Omnia, nunc primum collecta. Ed. Dutens, L. 6 vols. Geneva: Fratres des Tournes, 1768–1789.

Oeuvres de Leibniz. Ed. Foucher de Careil, A., 7 vols. Paris: Firmin Didot Frères: 1859–1875.

Gottfried Wilhelm Leibniz: Sämtliche Schriften und Briefe. Ed. Deutsche Akademie der Wissenschaften zu Berlin: Berlin, 1923– . Cited by series and volume.

Die Philosophischen Schriften von Leibniz. Ed. Gerhardt, C.I. 7 vols. Repr.; Hildesheim: Olms Verlag, 1978.

Der Briefwechsel des Gottfried Wilhelm Leibniz in der Königlichen Öffentlichen Bibliothek zu Hannover. Ed. Bodemann, E. Repr.; Hildesheim: Olms Verlag, 1966.

Die Leibniz-Handschriften des Königlichen Öffentlichen Bibliothek zu Hannover. Ed. Bodemann, E. Repr.; Hildesheim: Olms Verlag, 1966.

Other Sources

Allen, D., (ed.). *Leibniz:* *Theodicy* (Abridged). Indianapolis: Bobbs-Merrill, 1966.

Beck, L.W. *Early German Philosophy.* Cambridge, MA: Harvard University Press, 1969.

Bernard, Henri. "Chu Hsi's Philosophy and Its Interpretation by Leibniz." *Tien Hsia Monthly,* V (1937).

Bloom, Irene, trans. and ed. *Knowledge Painfully Acquired: the K'un-chih chi* (by Lo Ch'in-shun). New York: Columbia University Press, 1987.

Bodde, Derk. "Harmony and Conflict in Chinese Philosophy." *Studies in Chinese Thought,* ed. Arthur F. Wright. Chicago: University of Chicago Press, 1953.

Bornet, P. "La Préface des *Novissima Sinica." Monumenta Serica,* XV (1956).

Cammann, Schuyler. "The Origin of Trigram Circles in Ancient China." *Bulletin of the Museum of Far Eastern Antiquities,* LXII (1990).

Chan Wing-tsit. (1) "The Evolution of the Neo-Confucian Concept of *Li* As Principle." *The Tsing Hua Journal of Chinese Studies,* new series, IV (1964).

———. (2) ed. *Chu Hsi and Neo-Confucianism.* Honolulu: University Press of Hawaii, 1986.

Ching, Julia, and Oxtoby, Willard, eds. (1) *Discovering China.* Rochester, NY: University of Rochester Press, 1992.

———. (2) *Moral Enlightenment: Leibniz and Wolff on China.* Monumenta Serica Monograph Series, Volume XXVI. Nettetal: Steyler Verlag, 1992.

von Collani, C. (1) "Leibniz und die chinesische Ritenstreit." *Leibniz: Tradition und Aktualitaet.* V. Internationaler Leibniz-Kongress: Hannover, 14–19 November 1988. Hannover: G.W. Leibniz Gesellschaft, 1988.

———. (2) *P. Joachim Bouvet S.J.: Sein Leben und Sein Werk.* Monumenta Serica Monograph Series, Volume XVII. Nettetal: Steyler Verlag, 1985.

Collins, J. *The Thomistic Philosophy of the Angels.* Washington: Catholic University of America Press, 1947.

Cook, D. (1) "Metaphysics, Politics and Ecumenism: Leibniz' *Discourse on the Natural Theology of the Chinese." Studia Leibnitiana,* Supplement XIX, 1980.

———. (2) "Review of *G.W. Leibniz: Novissima Sinica."* German trans. and ed. H. Reinbothe and H.-G. Nesselrath, *Monumenta Serica* XXXIV (1979–1980).

Cook, D., and Rosemont, H. (1) trans. and eds. *G.W. Leibniz: Discourse on the Natural Theology of the Chinese.* Honolulu: University Press of Hawaii, 1977; 1980.

―――. (2) "The Pre-Established Harmony Between Leibniz and Chinese Thought." *The Journal of the History of Ideas,* XLII (1981). Reprinted in Ching and Oxtoby (1).

Couturat, Louis. *La Logique de Leibniz.* Reprint; Hildesheim: Olms, 1961.

Creel, Herrlee G. (1) "Was Confucius Agnostic?" *T'oung Pao,* XXIX (1932).

―――. (2) *Confucius and the Chinese Way.* New York: Harper Torchbooks, 1960.

Cronin, Vincent. *The Wise Man from the West.* London: R. Hart-Davis, 1955.

Cross, F. L., ed. *The Oxford Dictionary of the Christian Church.* London: Oxford University Press, 1954.

Cummins, J.S., ed. *The Travels and Controversies of Friar Domingo Navarette.* 2 vols. London: The Hakluyt Society, 1962.

deBary, Wm. T. (1) "Some Common Tendencies in Neo-Confucianism." In *Confucianism in Action.* Ed. David S. Nivison and Arthur F. Wright. Stanford, CA: Stanford University Press, 1959.

―――. (2) ed. *The Unfolding of Neo-Confucianism.* New York City: Columbia University Press, 1975.

De Groot, J.J.M. *The Religious System of China.* 6 vols. Taipei: Ch'eng-wen Reprint Co., 1969.

Dehergne, J. *Répertoire des Jésuites de la Chine de 1552 à 1800.* Rome and Paris: Gregorian University Press, 1973.

d'Elia, Pasquale. *Galileo in China.* Cambridge, MA: Harvard University Press, 1960.

Descartes, R. *Meditations on First Philosophy.* Trans. Cress, D. Indianapolis, IN: Hackett, 1979.

Dictionnaire de Théologie Catholique. 15 vols. Paris: Letouzey et Ané, 1930.

Dimberg, Ronald. *The Life and Thought of Ho Hsin-yin.* Honolulu: University Press of Hawaii, 1974.

Dunne, George H., S.J. *Generation of Giants: The Story of the Jesuits in China in the Last Decades of the Ming Dynasty.* London: Routledge and Kegan Paul, 1962.

Duyvendak, J.J.L. "Early Chinese Studies in Holland." *T'oung P'ao,* XXXII (1936).

Eckert, H. *G.W. Leibniz' Scriptores Rerum Brunsvicensium.* Entstehung und Historiographische Bedeutung. Frankfurt: V. Klostermann, 1971.

Edwards, P., ed. *The Encyclopedia of Philosophy.* 8 vols. New York: Macmillan, 1967.

Farrer, Austin, ed., and Huggard, E.M., trans. *Leibniz: Theodicy.* La Salle, IL: Open Court, 1988.

Fingarette, Herbert. *Confucius—The Secular as Sacred.* New York: Harper and Row, 1972.

Frémont, C., G. W. Leibniz: *Discours sur la théologie naturelle des Chinois.* Paris: L'Herne, 1987.

Fung Yu-lan. *History of Chinese Philosophy.* 2 vols. Trans. Derk Bodde. Princeton, NJ: Princeton University Press, 1952.

Gernet, Jacques. *China and the Christian Impact.* Trans. Janet Lloyd. Cambridge: Cambridge University Press, 1985.

Gould, Stephen Jay. *Eight Little Piggies: Reflections in Natural History.* New York: Norton, 1993.

Graham, Angus. (1) *Disputes of the Tao.* La Salle, IL: Open Court, 1988.

———. (2) *Two Chinese Philosophers.* La Salle, IL: Open Court, 1992.

Hall, David, and Ames, Roger. *Thinking Through Confucius.* Albany, NY: SUNY Press, 1987.

Heeren, J.I. "Father Bouvet's Picture of Emperor K'ang Hsi." *Asia Major.* VII (1932).

Heyndrickx, Jerome, ed. *Philippe Couplet, S.J.* (1623–1693). Monumenta Serica Monograph Series. Volume XXII. Nettetal: Steyler Verlag, 1990.

Hoffman, E., and Klibansky, R., eds. *Nicolaus Cusanus: De Docta Ignorantia.* Leipzig: F. Meiner, 1932.

Karlgren, Bernhard. (1) *Grammata Serica.* Taipei: Ch'eng-wen Reprint Co., 1966.

———. (2) trans., *The Book of Documents.* Stockholm: Museum of Far Eastern Antiquities, 1950.

———. (3) trans., *The Book of Odes.* Stockholm: Museum of Far Eastern Antiquities, 1950.

Keightley, David. *Sources of Shang History: The Oracle-Bone Inscriptions of Bronze Age China.* Berkeley: University of California Press, 1979.

Klutstein-Rojtman, I., and Werblowsky, Z., trans. "Leibniz: De cultu Confucii civili: Du culte civique de Confucius." *Studia Leibnitiana,* XVI (1984).

Lach, Donald F. (1) ed. *The Preface to Leibniz' Novissima Sinica.* Honolulu: University Press of Hawaii, 1957.

————. (2) "Leibniz and China." *The Journal of the History of Ideas,* VI (1945). Reprinted in Ching and Oxtoby (1).

————. (3) "The Chinese Studies of Andreas Müller." *The Journal of the American Oriental Society,* LX (1940).

————. (4) *Asia and the Making of Europe.* Four volumes in several parts. Chicago: University of Chicago Press, 1965– .

Legge, James, trans. (1) *The Chinese Classics.* 2nd rev. ed. 7 vols. Shanghai, 1894.

————. (2) Li Chi: *Book of Rites.* 2 vols., with a new Introduction by C. and W. Chai. New Hyde Park: University Books, 1967.

Loemker, L., trans. and ed. *G.W. Leibniz: Philosophical Papers and Letters.* 2nd ed. Dordrecht: D. Reidel, 1976.

Longobardi, Nicholas. *De Confucio Ejusque Doctrina Tractatus.* Paris: 1701. (Published only in French in Dutens and Kortholt.)

Loosen, R., and Vonessen, F., trans. and eds. *Gottfried Wilhelm Leibniz: Zwei Briefe über das binäre Zahlensystem und die chinesische Philosophie.* Stuttgart: Belser-Presse, 1968.

Lundbaek, Knud. "The Image of Neo-Confucianism in *Confucius Sinarum Philosophus.*" *The Journal of the History of Ideas,* XLIV (1983). Reprinted in Ching and Oxtoby (1).

Malebranche, Nicholas. *Dialogue Between a Christian Philosopher and a Chinese Philosopher on the Existence and Nature of God.* Trans. A. Dominick Iorio. Washington D.C.: University Press of America, 1980.

Merkel, F.R. *G.W. Leibniz und die China-Mission.* Eine Untersuchung über die Anfaenge der protestantische Missionsbewegung. Leipzig: Hinrichs, 1920.

Metzger, Thomas. *Escape from Predicament.* New York City: Columbia University Press, 1977.

Meyer, R.W. *Leibnitz and the Seventeenth-Century Revolution.* Cambridge, England: Bowes and Bowes, 1952.

Mungello, David. (1) *Leibniz and Confucianism: The Search for Accord.* Honolulu: University Press of Hawaii, 1977.

————. (2) *Curious Land: Jesuit Accommodation and the Origins of Sinology.* Stuttgart: Franz Steiner Verlag, 1985.

————. (3) "Malebranche and Chinese Philosophy." *The Journal of the History of Ideas,* XLI (1980). Reprinted in Ching and Oxtoby (1).

Needham, Joseph. *Science and Civilisation in China.* 7 vols. Cambridge: Cambridge University Press, 1954– .

Nesselrath, H.-G., and Reinbothe, H., eds. and trans. *G.W. Leibniz: Novissima Sinica: Das Neueste von China (1697).* Cologne: Deutsche China-Gesellschaft, 1979.

New Catholic Encyclopaedia. 16 vols. New York: McGraw Hill, 1967.

Nivison, David S. "Protest Against Conventions and Conventions of Protest." In *The Confucian Persuasion,* ed. Arthur F. Wright. Stanford: Stanford University Press, 1960.

Parkinson, G.H., ed. *Leibniz: Philosophical Writings.* Rev. ed. London: J. M. Dent, 1973.

Peters, F. E. *Greek Philosophical Terms: A Historical Lexicon.* New York: New York University Press, 1967.

Pfister, Louis. *Notices biographiques et bibliographiques sur les Jésuites de l'ancienne mission de Chine 1552–1773.* 2 vols. Nendeln, Lichtenstein: Kraus Reprint, 1971.

Plato's Epistles. Trans. G. Murrow. Indianapolis: Bobbs-Merrill, 1962.

Quasten, J. *Patrology.* 3 vols. Utrecht: Spectrum, 1950.

Rescher, Nicholas. *The Philosophy of Leibniz.* Englewood Cliffs: Prentice-Hall, 1967.

Riley, P. "An Unpublished Lecture by Leibniz on the Greeks as Founders of Rational Theology: Its Relation to His 'Universal Jurisprudence.'" *The Journal of the History of Philosophy,* XIV (1976).

Rolt, C.E. *Dionysius the Areopagite on the Divine Names and the Mystical Theology.* New York: Macmillan, 1951.

Rosemont, Henry, Jr. (1) "Review Article: Herbert Fingarette's *Confucius—The Secular as Sacred.*" *Philosophy East and West.* XXVI (1976).

———. (2) "Rights vs. Rituals." In *Rules, Rituals, and Responsibility: Essays Dedicated to Herbert Fingarette,* ed. Mary I. Bockover. La Salle, IL: Open Court, 1992.

Rowbotham, A.L. *Missionary and Mandarin.* Reprint; New York: Russell and Russell, 1966.

Roy, Olivier. *Leibniz et la Chine.* Paris: J. Vrin, 1972.

Russell, Bertrand. *A Critical Exposition of the Philosophy of Leibniz.* Cambridge: Cambridge University Press, 1900.

Sainte-Marie, Antoine de [Antonio Caballero a Santa Maria]. *Traité sur quelques points importants de la Mission de la Chine.* Paris, 1701. (In Dutens and Kortholt.)

Schneweis, E. *Angels and Demons according to Lactantius.* Washington: Catholic University of American Press, 1944.

Schrecker, P., and Schrecker, Anne, trans. and eds. *Leibniz: Monadology and Other Philosophical Essays.* Indianapolis: Bobbs-Merrill, 1965.

Schwartz, Benjamin. (1) "Some Polarities in Confucian Thought." In *Confucianism in Action,* ed. David S. Nivison and Arthur F. Wright. Stanford: Stanford University Press, 1959.

―――. (2) *The World of Thought in Ancient China.* Cambridge MA: Harvard University Press, 1985.

Secret, F. "Quand La Kabbale Expliquait le 'Yi King' ou un Aspect Oublié du Figuratisme du P. Joachim Bouvet." *Revue de l'Histoire des Religions,* CXCV (1979).

Sivin, Nathan. (1) "Copernicus in China." *Studia Copernicana,* VI (1973).

―――. (2) *Cosmos and Computation in Early Chinese Mathematical Astronomy.* Leiden: E. J. Brill, 1969.

Sleigh, R. *Leibniz and Arnauld: A Commentary on Their Correspondence.* Yale University Press: New Haven, 1990.

Smith, D.E. *History of Mathematics.* 2 vols. Boston: Ginn and Co., 1925.

Spence, Jonathan. (1) *Emperor of China.* New York: Alfred Knopf, Inc., 1974.

―――. (2) *The Memory Palace of Matteo Ricci.* New York: Viking Penguin, 1984.

Swiderski, R.M. "Bouvet and Leibniz: A Scholarly Correspondence." *Eighteenth Century Studies,* XIV (1980).

Tillman, Hoyt C. *Chen Liang on Public Interest and the Law.* Honolulu: University Press of Hawaii, 1994.

Toulmin, Stephen. *Cosmopolis: the Hidden Agenda of Modernity.* New York: Free Press, 1990.

Treadgold, Donald W. *The West in Russia and China.* vol. 2: *China 1582–1949.* Cambridge: Cambridge University Press, 1973.

Trigault, Nicola, S.J. *China in the 16th Century: The Journals of Matteo Ricci.* Trans. L.J. Gallagher, S.J. New York: Random House, 1953.

Tu Wei-ming. *Humanity and Self-Cultivation: Essays in Confucian Thought.* Berkeley: Asian Humanities Press, 1979.

Van Den Wyngaert, A., ed. *Sinica Franciscana.* 16 vols. in 8. Collegium S. Bonaventurae, 1929–1936.

Van Kley, Edwin J., and Pullapilly, Cyriac K. *Asia and the West: Encounters and Exchanges from the Age of Explorations.* Notre Dame, IN: Cross Cultural Publication Co., 1986.

Vaeth, Alfons, S.J. *Johann Adam Schall von Bell S.J.* Monumenta Serica Monograph Series, Volume XXV. Nettetal: Steyler Verlag, 1991.

Waley, Arthur. (1) "Leibniz and Fu Hsi." *Bulletin of the London School of Oriental Studies,* II (1929).

———. (2) trans. *The Book of Songs.* New York: Grove Press, 1960.

———. (3) trans. *The Analects of Confucius.* New York: Modern Library, n.d.

Walker, D.P. *The Ancient Theology.* Ithaca, NY: Cornell University Press, 1972.

Werner, E.T.C., ed. *Dictionary of Chinese Mythology.* Shanghai: Kelly and Walsh, Ltd. 1932.

Widmaier, R. (1) *Die Rolle der Chinesischen Schrift in Leibniz' Zeichentheorie.* Wiesbaden: Franz Steiner Verlag, 1983.

———. (2) ed. *Leibniz korrespondiert mit China.* Der Briefwechsel mit den Jesuitenmissionaren (1689–1714). Frankfurt: V. Klostermann, 1990.

Wiener, Philip P. (1) ed., *Leibniz: Selections.* New York: Charles Scribner's Sons, 1951.

———. (2) "On Philosophical Synthesis." *Philosophy East and West,* XII (1963).

Wilhelm, Hellmut. (1) "Leibniz and the I Ching." *Collectanea Commissiones Synodalis,* XVI (1943).

———. (2) *Change: Eight Lectures on the I Ching.* New York: Pantheon Books, 1960.

Wittkower, R. *Architectural Principles in the Age of Humanism.* New York: Random House, 1965.

Wright, Arthur F. *Buddhism in Chinese History.* New York: Atheneum, 1965.

Zacher, H.J. *Die Hauptschriften zur Dyadik von G.W. Leibniz, Ein Beitrag zur Geschichte des binären Zahlensystem.* Frankfurt: V. Klostermann, 1973.

Zangger, Christian D. *Welt und Konversation.* Die theologische Begründung der Mission bei G.W. Leibniz. Zurich: Theologischer Verlag, 1973.

Zeller, E. (1) *Outlines of the History of Greek Philosophy.* 13 ed. rev.; New York: Russell and Russell, 1962.

———. (2) *The Stoics, Epicureans and Skeptics.* Rev. ed.; New York: Russell and Russell, 1962.

Zempliner, Arthur. "Gedanken über die erste deutsche Übersetzung von Leibniz' Abhandlung über die chinesische Philosophie." In *Studia Leibnitiana,* II (1970).

Name Index

Subject Index

also Longobardi, Ricci
Mission Treatise, 15, 28, 33, 67, 76ff, 98n, 121n. *See also* Sainte-Marie
Missionaries, 2, 3, 5, 13–14, 18–19, 28–29, 49n, 51–53, 110, 119
  Catholic, 2–3, 6, 14, 101n
  Protestant, 2–3, 5.
  See also Dominicans, Franciscans, Jesuits, Longobardi, Ricci, Sainte-Marie
Monadology, xii, 116n, 117n
Monads, *xi,* 2, 7, 88n, 116n

Nan-lin (virtue of the Earth), 107
Natural Religion (civil order), 46, 51. *See also* Theology, Natural
Neo-Confucian period, 19
Neo-Confucianism, 26–29, 67n, 89n
Nestorian penetration of China, 18, 58, 64
Novissima Sinica, 4–5, 13, 16, 30, 45–59, 64

Order, 105
Order of Heaven, 102

Patriarchs, 98, 102n, 105
  contact with Chinese, 110
  See also Early Church Fathers
Pe (bo, material soul), 124–25. *See also* Soul
Phaedo, 108, 126n, 127n
Phaedrus, 127n
Philosophical Summa, 122
Pian (sacrifice), 115, 124n
Portuguese, 53–54
Pre-Socratics, 117
Primal air 90–93. *See also Li, Matter, Qi*
Prime Matter, 7, 37, 83–86, 90, 96, 128
  Passive vs. Active Character, 83–86, 89
  See also Li, Qi

Principles of Nature and Grace, 117n
Purgatory, 125, 132

Qi (air), 68, 72, 77, 90, 93, 97–99, 107, 128
Qun shen (hosts of spirits), 124n

Reason, Sovereign, 105. *See also Li*
Religion Treatise, 14, 28, 33, 42, 69, 76ff, 88n, 106n. *See also* Longobardi
Revelation, Biblical, 17
Rites, Chinese, 32, 61–64, 70. *See also* Ancestors, *Li,* Sacrifice
Rites Controversy, 3–5, 9, 67n
Ritual Practice, of Shang and Zhou, 26
Romans, and Arithmetic, 135
Rome (Papal Seat), 52

Sacrifice, 120–23
  to Ancestors. *See* Ancestor Worship
  and Social Status, 123–24
  to Spirits, 114
Sage Kings, 8, 19–20, 23–24, 114, 125–27, 131–32. *See also* individual kings such as *Fuxi, Xun, Yao*
Scholastics, 7, 75, 77, 86, 89, 96n, 110–11, 113–14
Schoolmen. *See* Scholastics
Self-cultivation, Chinese Belief in, 27
Shang Di, 3, 32, 64, 69–70, 74, 84–85, 92, 99, 101–2, 104–11, 115, 117, 119, 121n, 122, 124–27, 129–31
  as Governor of the World, 122
  as Heaven, 107
  and *Li* are same thing, 102
  Sainte-Marie's Views on, 84–85, 103
  and *Taiji,* 108
  See also God, *Tian*